بسم الله الرحمن الرحيم

THE REMEMBRANCE OF GOD

THE REMEMBRANCE OF GOD

The Outcome of Contemplation over Loud *Dhikr*

(*Natījatu al-fikr fīl-jahri bil-dhikr*)

IMAM JALĀL AL-DĪN AL-SUYŪṬĪ

Translated by
SAJEDA MARYAM POSWAL

Revised with Notes, Biography and Appendices by
GIBRIL FOUAD HADDAD

AMAL PRESS
BRISTOL • ENGLAND

Amal Press, PO Box 688, Bristol BS99 3ZR, England

http://www.amalpress.com
info@amalpress.com

 A CIP catalogue record for this book is available from the British Library

Manufactured in the United States of America

ISBN 978-0-9552359-5-5 paperback

Special thanks to the Cordoba Financial Group.

CORDOBA
FINANCIAL GROUP

CONTENTS

Acknowledgements ix

Publisher's Note xi

Abbreviations xv

Biography of Imam al-Suyūṭī 1

The Remembrance of God 19

APPENDICES:

- I. Published works of al-Suyūṭī 35
- II. Ḥanafī Fatwas on Loud *Dhikr* in the Mosque 45
- III. *Dhikr* "Allah, Allah" 53

NOTES 59

BIBLIOGRAPHY 79

BIOGRAPHICAL NOTES 85

ACKNOWLEDGEMENTS

THE TRANSLATION OF Imam al-Suyūṭī's fatwa originally appeared in *Dhikr-i-Ilāhi*[*] ("Recollection of Allah the Almighty") a compilation by the late shaykh, Haḍrat Abū Anīs Muḥammad Barkat 'Alī (may Allah bless him) consisting of the commandments of Allah and the sayings of the Prophet Muḥammad ﷺ to *Remember Allah with much remembrance* (Qur'an 33:40–41).

We thank Dār-ul-Ehsān and Hajī Imdād Aḥmad Poswal in particular for allowing us to reproduce this invaluable text.

We would also like to thank the Cordoba Financial Group, who through their generous donation enabled us to publish this legal treatise.

[*] Huddersfield, UK: Dār-ul-Ehsān, 2000.

PUBLISHER'S NOTE

WE LIVE IN a time when there is a growing interest in understanding Islam not only by Muslims but also by people of other faiths and even by people of no faith. Books that were once available only in the Arabic language are being translated into English, though as yet these translations represent only a scant fraction of the realms of knowledge open for us to explore. While Muslim scholars, sages, and legal experts often expounded their philosophies in multi-volume epics,[1] no comparison could be found in medieval Europe. It is the intention of Amal Press to make available to people in the West these illuminating texts that have been taught and passed down from teacher to student for generations in the Muslim lands.

Far from being the torchbearers of intellectual inquiry, the Muslim world of today bears little resemblance to the past civilization that so many Muslims passionately talk of. The Islamic discourse is highly politicized, leaving ethical, moral, and spiritual dimensions to become marginalized and neglected. It is because of this remarkable contrast between the classical period and the modern that Amal Press seeks to address the reasons for the current state of malaise in the Muslim world. One thing is certain: the Islamic discourse of the past was never determined by those whose mission was to destroy and wreak havoc. Whereas classical Islam offered a religion to live for, contemporary expressions of Islam seem to create a religion to die for. It is no coincidence that such proponents or movements do not have scholars in their ranks, nor do they produce anything near the intellectual output of their spiritual forefathers.

The Islamic tradition is rooted in knowledge that is carried and transmitted by inheritors of the prophets who possess a light in their hearts, a light that is passed on to others; illuminating and intoxicating all those who come into contact with it. Tragically, this divine gift has become mutated and distorted, so rather than seeking enlightenment from its deep spiritual tradition, some Muslims have transformed Islam into a rabid ideology—one that hardens the hearts and is unable to provide equilibrium in the turmoil and agitation that surrounds us all. These modern manifestations of Islam are quick to condemn the West, but they embrace its technology and readily use its weapons of mass destruction.

Dhikr, that is the remembrance of God,[2] is the cure for forgetfulness. While humankind was created weak, constantly falling and slipping into a state of heedlessness, prophets were sent to *remind* humankind of their divine spark and the ability to reach great heights; to be great people and transcend their lower desires.

This publication is a translation of a legal response (fatwa) to a specific question on "Remembering God" (*dhikr* Allah) aloud and in a group of people. Written by the renowned Egyptian scholar, historian, biographer, hadith master, jurist, and probably one of the most prolific of all medieval Muslim scholars, Jalāl al-Dīn al-Suyūṭī (d. 911/1505) it should decisively end all disputes surrounding a blessed act of communal worship.

At a time when people of violence are invoking God, we learn from this major scholar the benefits of remembering God and chanting His names. Its effect is to instill tranquility and a sense of calm within the one who recites blessed words, qualities that seems to be absent from many people today. Were people to remain in the state they achieve through *dhikr*, the Prophet Muḥammad ﷺ said that, "The angels would come to see you to the point that they would greet you in the middle of the road."[3]

In countless prophetic traditions (hadiths), we are told how the remembrance of God is "the best of all deeds," and how gatherings of *dhikr* are akin to both the "gardens of paradise," and the "gatherings of angels." It comes as no surprise that when the Prophet Muḥammad ﷺ was asked, "Which of the servants of God is best in rank before Him on the day of resurrection?" he responded, "The ones who remember Him much."[4] The heart that pulsates to the testimony of God's majesty begins to rust through the absence of the remembrance of God, and it is only *dhikr* that can once again "polish"[5] the hearts.

The state of the heart is of utmost importance for the believer, for it is neither the status of man nor his outward form that will be of any benefit to him on the day that all will be come to know the fruits of their actions, except that is, those who bring God *a sound heart* (Qur'an 26:88–89).

The purification of the heart is conditional on the purification of the tongue and while today many Muslims seek to enrich the mind, they do so to the neglect of the heart. Too few know the science of the attributes of the heart and thus fail to recognize the praiseworthy and blameworthy traits. Our tongues speak with such carelessness and impunity that we fail to understand the consequences. How often did the Prophet ﷺ say to guard and restrain our tongues? His advice was to use it only to speak good (or to remain silent)[6] and to keep it busy with the remembrance of God.[7] The heart is the core of the human creature and it is by constant *dhikr* that it becomes trained, humbled, and purified.

ABBREVIATIONS

'Abd b. Ḥumayd = 'Abd b. Ḥumayd's *Musnad*
'Abd al-Razzāq = 'Abd al-Razzāq's *Muṣannaf*
Abū Dāwūd = Abū Dāwūd's *Sunan*
Abū Nu'aym = Abū Nu'aym's *Ḥilyat al-awliyā'*
Abū Ya'lā = Abū Ya'lā's *Musnad*
Aḥmad = Aḥmad's *Musnad*
al-Bazzār = al-Bazzār's *Musnad*
al-Bukhārī = al-Bukhārī's *Ṣaḥīḥ*
al-Dārimī = al-Dārimī's *Musnad*
al-Ḥākim = al-Ḥākim's *Mustadrak*
al-Haythamī = al-Haythamī's *Majma' al-zawā'id*
Ibn Abī Shayba = Ibn Abī Shayba's *Muṣannaf*
Ibn Ḥibbān = *Ṣaḥīḥ.Ibn Ḥibbān*
Ibn Khuzayma = Ibn Khuzayma's *Ṣaḥīḥ*
Ibn Mājah = Ibn Mājah's *Sunan*
Ibn Sa'd = Ibn Sa'd's *Ṭabaqāt al-kubrā*
al-Mundhirī = al-Mundhirī's *al-Targhīb wal-tarhīb*
Muslim = Muslim's *Ṣaḥīḥ*
al-Nasā'ī = al-Nasā'ī's [Minor] *Sunan* (*al-Mujtabā*)
al-Ṭabarī = al-Ṭabarī's *Tafsīr*
al-Ṭayālisī = al-Ṭayālisī's *Musnad*
al-Tirmidhī = al-Tirmidhī's *Sunan*

BIOGRAPHY OF IMAM AL-SUYŪṬĪ

(*849–911/1443–1505*)

ABD AL-RAḤMĀN B. Kamāl al-Dīn Abī Bakr b. Muḥammad b. Sābiq al-Dīn, Jalāl al-Dīn Abū al-Faḍl al-Miṣrī al-Suyūṭī al-Khuḍayrī al-Shāfi'ī, also known as Ibn al-Asyūṭī, one of the Friends of God and His Signs to creation, the *Mujtahid* Imam and Renewer of the ninth Islamic century, foremost hadith master, jurist, Sufi, philologist, Ash'arī theologian, and historian, he authored works in virtually every Islamic science.[1] Imam al-Suyūṭī is arguably the most famous link in a three-century (from the seventh to the tenth) teacher-student chain of several prestigious, major Shāfi'ī-Ash'arī imams, all of them jurists and hadith masters strongly inclined to *taṣawwuf*, beginning in Damascus then moving to Cairo, and ending in Makka al-Mukarrama:

al-Nawawī
|
al-Mizzī
|
al-Taqī al-Subkī and al-Sirāj al-Bulqīnī
|
Sāra and al-Tāj al-Subkī, al-'Alam al-Bulqīnī and al-Zayn al-'Irāqī
|
al-Walī al-'Irāqī, al-Bulqīnī the grandson and Ibn Ḥajar al-'Asqalānī
|
al-Sakhāwī, al-Suyūṭī and Zakariyyā al-Anṣārī
|
Ibn Ḥajar al-Haytamī

All of them have been called Shaykh al-Islam.

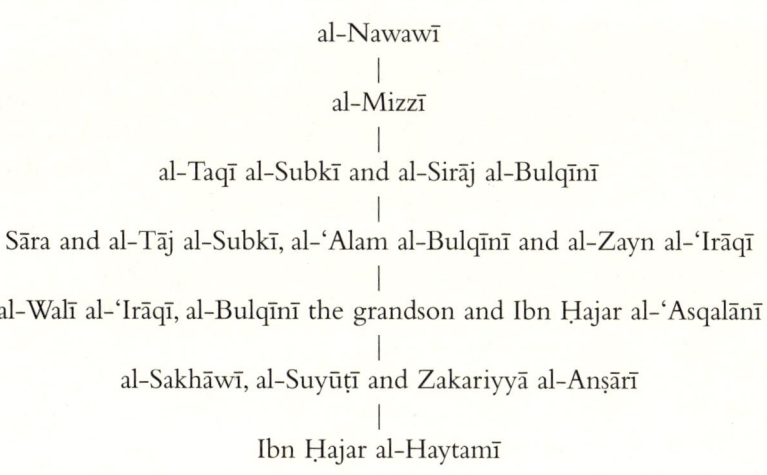

Biographies and Autobiographies

The five earliest sources for al-Suyūṭī's life are his two autobiographical notices in *Ḥusn al-muḥāḍara* and *al-Taḥadduth bi-ni'mat Allāh*, the fourth volume of al-Sakhāwī's *al-Ḍaw' al-lāmi'*, 'Abd al-Qādir al-'Aydarūsī's, *al-Nūr al-sāfir 'an akhbār al-qarn al-'āshir,* and Najm al-Dīn al-Ghazzī's, *al-Kawākib al-sā'ira bi-a'yān al-mi'at al-'āshira.*

His Teachers

Al-Suyūṭī was born to a prestigious family of shaykhs, governors, and merchants. His mother was Turkish and his father of either Khuḍayrī-Baghdādī or non-Arab ancestry. Al-'Aydarūsī says that al-Suyūṭī's mother was fetching a book for his father at the time she entered labor and gave birth to him in the library, hence his nickname Ibn al-Kutub—Son of the Books. He was taken as a baby to the *maqām* of Sitt Nafīsa where one of the friends of God, Shaykh Muḥammad al-Majdhūb, supplicated for him. At the age of three, his father took him to the gathering of the peerless Shaykh al-Islam, the unequaled hadith Master of the Ages, Ibn Ḥajar al-'Asqalānī (773–852 AH) the year of the latter's death and obtained permission (*ijāza*) for 'Abd al-Raḥmān to narrate from him. Al-Suyūṭī said in his *Mu'jam* he went on to obtain hadith auditions (*sama'*) as well as permissions to narrate from about a hundred and fifty shaykhs, "but I did not do much of hadith audition (*samā' al-riwāya*) because I busied myself with what was more important, namely, the reading of its expertise (*qirā'at al-dirāya*)."

He lost his father at age six, in or around the year 855 AH and was raised as an orphan in Cairo under the tutelage of the Ḥanafī *mujtahid* al-Kamāl b. al-Humām as stipulated in his father's testament. He memorized the Qur'an at eight then Ibn Daqīq al-'Īd's *'Umdat al-aḥkām* which regroups all the hadiths that are fundamental to the study of the law, al-Nawawī's *Minhāj al-ṭālibīn*, al-Bayḍāwī's *Minhāj al-wuṣūl ilā 'ilm al-uṣūl*, and Ibn Mālik's *Alfiyya*, a thousand-line poem on Arabic grammar.

He devoted himself to studying the sacred sciences under the foremost teachers of his time, mostly Shāfi'īs and Ḥanafīs such as:

- Shaykh al-Islam Qadi al-quḍāt 'Alam al-Dīn Ṣāliḥ b. 'Umar al-Bulqīnī (d. 868 AH) who wrote the commendation (*taqrīẓ*) for al-Suyūṭī's very first work—an explanation of *isti'ādha* and *basmala* he wrote at age seventeen—and with whom he studied Shāfi'ī jurisprudence until his death two years later, then with his son (d. 878 AH) who gave him authorization to teach and give fatwa the year of his death, in al-Suyūṭī's twenty-seventh year, after which the latter studied with:
- Shaykh al-Islam Sharaf al-Dīn al-Munāwī, with whom he read *fiqh* and exegesis;
- Taqī al-Dīn al-Shumunnī al-Ḥanafī in hadith and the sciences of Arabic, who wrote him commendations on *Sharḥ alfiyyat Ibn Mālik* and *Jam' al-jawāmi'* in Arabic, with whom he stayed for four years until his death, and whom he helped correct his marginalia on 'Iyāḍ's *Shifā;*
- Shaykh Muḥyī al-Dīn al-Kāfiajī with whom he studied for fourteen years *tafsīr, uṣūl,* Arabic, philology, and others; he names him the Teacher of the Universe (*Ustādh al-wujūd*);
- The specialist in the principles of the law, Jalāl al-Dīn al-Maḥallī, together with whom he compiled perhaps the most widespread condensed commentary of Qur'an in our time, *Tafsīr al-jalālayn*;
- The Ḥanbalī Qadi al-Quḍāt 'Izz al-Dīn Aḥmad b. Ibrāhīm al-Kinānī who gave him the *kunya* Abū al-Faḍl;
- Burhān al-Dīn al-Biqā'ī against whom he differed sharply over *taṣawwuf;*
- Shams al-Dīn al-Sakhāwī with whom he had a great falling out;[2]
- The centenarian specialist of *farā'iḍ* Shihāb al-Dīn al-Shārumsāḥī; and
- The hadith master Sayf al-Dīn Qāsim b. Quṭlūbaghā.

His Travels

He travelled in the pursuit of knowledge to Damascus, the Ḥijāz, Yemen, India, Morocco, the lands south of Morocco, as well as to centers of learning in Egypt such as Maḥalla, Dumyāṭ, and Fayyūm. He was for some time head teacher of hadith at the Shaykhūniyya School in Cairo at the recommendation of Imam Kamāl al-Dīn b. al-Humām, then the Baybarsiyya, out of which he was divested through the complaints of disgruntled shaykhs, which he had replaced as teachers. He then retired into scholarly seclusion, never to go back to teaching.

His Retirement from the World at the Age of Forty

Ibn Iyās in *Tārīkh miṣr* states that when al-Suyūṭī reached forty years of age, he abandoned the company of men for the solitude of Rawḍat al-Miqyās by the bank of the Nile, avoiding his former colleagues as though he had never known them, and it was here that he authored most of his nearly six hundred books and treatises. Wealthy Muslims and princes would visit him with offers of money and gifts, but he put all of them off, and when the sultan requested his presence a number of times, he refused. He once said to the sultan's envoy: "Do not ever come back to us with a gift, for in truth God has put an end to all such needs for us."

His Works

The editors of the book, *A Guide to al-Suyūṭī's Manuscripts* have listed 723 works to al-Suyūṭī's name.[3] Some of these are brief fatwas which do not exceed four pages, like his notes on the hadith "Whoever says: 'I am knowledgeable,' he is ignorant"[4] titled *A'dhab al-manāhil fī ḥadīth man qāla anā 'ālim*; while others, like the *Itqān fī 'ulūm al-Qur'ān or Tadrīb al-rāwī*, are full-fledged tomes. His student and biographer, Shams al-Dīn al-Dāwūdī al-Mālikī—the author of *Ṭabaqāt al-mufassirīn al-kubrā*—said: "I saw the Shaykh with my own eyes writing and finishing three works in one day which he himself authored and proofread. At the same time he was dictating hadith and replying beautifully to whatever was brought to his attention." Sakhāwī reproached him his plagiarism of past books, and others said that the profusion of his works made for their lack of completion and frequent flaws and contradictions. This is a charge commonly laid at the door of prolific authors, such as Ibn al-Jawzī and Aḥmad b. Taymiyya.

Blessed with success in his years of solitude, it is difficult to name a field in which al-Suyūṭī did not make outstanding contributions, among them his thirty-volume hadith encyclopedia *Jamʿ al-jawāmiʿ* [The collection of collections]; his exegesis *Tafsīr al-jalālayn* [Commentary of the two jalals], of which he finished the second half of an uncompleted manuscript by Jalāl al-Dīn Maḥallī in just forty days; his classic commentary on the sciences of hadith, *Tadrīb al-rāwī fī sharḥ taqrīb al-Nawawī* [The training of the hadith transmitter: a commentary on al-Nawawī's "Facilitation"]; and many others. He produced a sustained output of scholarly writings until his death at the age of sixty-two. He was buried in Ḥawsh Qawṣūn in Cairo.

His Hadith Mastery

Al-Shaʿrānī in *al-Ṭabaqāt al-ṣughrā* mentioned that al-Suyūṭī said he memorized two hundred thousand hadiths and added: "If there were more, I would have memorized them, and there might not be more than that on the face of the earth."[5] Al-Suyūṭī had called Ibn Ḥajar, "the absolute hadith master of the world" and said: "Hadith scholars today depend on four figures in the field of narrator-criticism and other related fields: al-Mizzī, al-Dhahabī, al-ʿIrāqī, and Ibn Ḥajar."[6] He relates that during pilgrimage, Ibn Ḥajar drank *zamzam* water and petitioned to reach the level of al-Dhahabī in hadith, which he subsequently "reached and surpassed" according to al-Suyūṭī, to the point that he was nicknamed "the second Bayhaqī." Al-Suyūṭī said: "When I went on hajj I drank *zamzam* water to several intentions. Among them: that I reach, in *fiqh*, the level of Shaykh Sirāj al-Dīn al-Bulqīnī and, in hadith, that of the *ḥāfiẓ* Ibn Ḥajar."[7] In a later work he states: "There is not in our time, on the face of the earth, from east to west, anyone more knowledgeable than myself in hadith and the Arabic language, save al-Khaḍir or the pole of saints or some other *walī*—none of whom I include in my statement—and God knows best."[8]

Al-Suyūṭī also built on al-Dhahabī's masterpiece biographical dictionary, *Tadhkirat al-ḥuffāẓ* [The memorial of the hadith masters], without peer in Islamic literature, a chronological history of the synchronical layers of the hadith masters beginning with Abū Bakr al-Ṣiddīq and ending with al-Mizzī, al-Dhahabī's teacher. Most of the 1176 entries contain, in addition to biographical data, a hadith transmitted to al-Dhahabī through a chain containing the entry's subject. Ibn Ḥajar received it from Abū Hurayra b. al-Dhahabī.[9] Al-Suyūṭī condensed and updated it in *Ṭabaqāt al-ḥuffāẓ*, adding 56 more entries, followed by others.[10]

Al-Suyūṭī also wrote an illustrious two-volume commentary on al-Nawawī's *al-Taqrīb wal-taysīr li-maʿrifati sunan al-bashīr al-nadhīr*—an abridgment of al-Nawawī's own *Irshād*, itself a commentary on Ibn al-Ṣalāḥ's *ʿUlūm al-ḥadīth*—which al-Suyūṭī titled *Tadrīb al-rāwī fī sharḥ taqrīb al-Nawāwī* and which went on to become a classic textbook that is required reading in the sciences of hadith.

His Mastery of the Qurʾanic Sciences

As in the sphere of hadith, al-Suyūṭī built on Ibn Ḥajar's work in *tafsīr* and the Qurʾanic sciences as well. In *al-Iḥkām li-bayān mā fīl-Qurʾān min al-ibhām*, also named *Mubhamāt al-Qurʾān*, Ibn Ḥajar had collated al-Suhaylī's[11] *al-Taʿrīf wal-iʿlām fīmā ubhima fīl-Qurʾān min al-asmāʾ wal-aʿlām* and its supplement by Ibn ʿAsākir, *Dhayl al-taʿrīf wal-iʿlām*, works devoted to the identification of unnamed references in the Qurʾan, to which al-Suyūṭī added his *Mufḥimāt al-aqrān fī mubhamāt al-Qurʾān* [Silencing the peers concerning the omissions of the Qurʾan].

Ibn Ḥajar had also authored a poem listing the non-Arabic words of the Qurʾan and completing a similar work by Tāj al-Dīn b. al-Subkī, to which al-Suyūṭī added more in his two works *Mutawakkilī fīmā warada fīl-Qurʾān bil-lughat al-ḥabashiyya wal-fārisiyya wal-rūmiyya wal-hindiyya wal-siryāniyya wal-ʿibrāniyya wal-nabaṭiyya wal-qibṭiyya wal-turkiyya wal-zanjiyya wal-barbariyya* [My reliance concerning what was mentioned in the Qurʾan in Ethiopian, Farsi, Greek, Hindī, Syriac, Hebrew, Nabatean, Coptic, Turkic, African, and Berber] and *al-Muhadhdhab fīmā waqaʿa fīl-Qurʾān min al-muʿarrab* [The emendation concerning the foreign words and phrases in the Qur'an], listing a total of over a hundred words and expressions. His *Durr al-manthūr fil-tafsīr al-ma'thūr* represents the most voluminous hadith-based commentary of the Qur'an in later times after the unsurpassed efforts of al-Ṭabarī and al-Baghawī.

Al-Suyūṭī authored *al-Itqān fī 'ulūm al-Qur'ān*, a systematic encyclopedia of the obligatory Qur'anic sciences which every narrator of commentary and exegete must master. This book ranks among the classics of the genre beginning with the early works of *Faḍā'il al-Qur'ān*, then the two great "etiquette of the Qur'an" works by al-Qurṭubī and al-Nawawī, finally the large manuals by al-Zarkashī and al-Zarqānī.

In the *Itqān* al-Suyūṭī cites from al-Ṭabarī's *Tafsīr* a seminal narration of Ibn 'Abbās on hermeneutical principles: "There are four aspects of explication: an aspect Arabs know from their language, an exegesis that no one is excused for being ignorant of, an exegesis known to the scholars, and an exegesis no one knows except God." Our teacher, Nūr al-Dīn 'Itr, comments in his own manual titled *'Ulūm al-Qur'ān*:

> This is a sound and fine division. The explication that Arabs know by their language goes back to the Arabic language, including philology, grammatical analysis, and various disciplines of Arabic linguistics. The explication no one is excused for not knowing is what is patent to anyone endowed with understanding. The explication the scholars know goes back to their personal reasoning (*ijtihād*) and precisely deducing the Qur'an's finer points, including its hidden meanings, rhetorical style, legal judgments, and other specialized disciplines. As for the fourth division, it is what is associated with the reality of the unseen, e.g., the angels and souls; knowing it as it truly is, is resigned to God Most High.[12]

His Taṣawwuf

Al-Suyūṭī's chain of transmission in *taṣawwuf* goes back to Shaykh 'Abd al-Qādir al-Jīlānī and he belonged to the Shādhilī *ṭarīqa,* which he eulogized in two monographs defending *taṣawwuf, Itḥāf al-firqa bi-rafwi al-khirqa* [The gift to the group in the mending of the cloak] and *Ta'yīd al-ḥaqīqat al-'aliyya wa-tashyīd al-ṭarīqat al-shādhiliyyah* [The support of the higher truth and the strengthening of the Shādhilī path]. In the latter book he states: "I have looked at the matters which the imams of Sharia have criticized in Sufis, and I did not see a single true Sufi holding such positions. Rather, they are held by the people of innovation and the extremists who have claimed for themselves the title of Sufi while in reality they are not Sufis." In the *Tashyīd* he also produces narrative chains of transmission proving that al-Ḥasan al-Baṣrī did in fact narrate directly from 'Alī b. Abī Ṭālib ﷺ. This goes against commonly received opinion among the scholars of hadith[13] although it was also reported as the opinion of Imam Aḥmad b. Ḥanbal.[14]

Al-Suyūṭī gave *taṣawwuf* his *Ḥāwī lil-fatāwī,* which contains legal proofs and precedents on many issues connected to Sufism and helped the Sufis reply to their objectors and show that the practices of *taṣawwuf* were part and parcel of Islam, among them the fatwa proving the permissibility of loud *dhikr* in the mosques, translated as "*Remembering God: the outcome of contemplation over loud dhikr*" in this book. In another fatwa titled *al-Minḥa fīl-sibḥa* [The profit in *dhikr* beads], al-Suyūṭī recounts the story of 'Ikrima, who asked his teacher 'Umar al-Mālikī about *dhikr* beads. The latter replied that he had also asked his teacher al-Ḥasan al-Baṣrī about it and was told: "Something we have used at the beginning of the road we are not desirous to leave at the end. I love to remember God with my heart, my hand, and my tongue." Al-Suyūṭī comments: "And how should it be otherwise, when the *dhikr* beads remind one of God Most High, and a person seldom sees *dhikr* beads except he remembers God, which is among the greatest of its benefits?"[15] Al-Haytamī's later *Fatāwā ḥadīthiyya* perfects the design pioneered by al-Suyūṭī in defending the Sunni character of *taṣawwuf* among other important themes.

When one of his teachers, Burhān al-Dīn Ibrāhīm b. 'Umar al-Biqā'ī,[16] attacked Ibn 'Arabī in a tract titled *Tanbīh al-ghabī ilā takfīr Ibn 'Arabī* [Warning to the dolt that Ibn 'Arabī is an apostate], al-Suyūṭī countered with a tract entitled *Tanbīh al-ghabī fī tanzīh Ibn 'Arabī* [Warning to the dolt that Ibn 'Arabī is upright]. Both epistles have been published.[17] In his reply, al-Suyūṭī states that he considers

Ibn 'Arabī a Friend of God whose writings are forbidden to those who read them without first learning the technical terms used by the Sufis.[18] He cites from Ibn Ḥajar's list in *Anbā' al-ghumr*, among the trusted scholars who kept a good opinion of Ibn 'Arabī or counted him a *walī*: Ibn 'Aṭā' Allāh al-Sakandarī (d. 709 AH), al-Yāfi'ī (d. 678 AH), Ibn 'Abd al-Salām after the latter's meeting with al-Shādhilī, Shihāb al-Dīn Abū al-'Abbās Aḥmad b. Yaḥyā al-Malwī al-Tilimsānī (d. 776 AH), Sirāj al-Dīn Abū Ḥafṣ 'Umar b. Isḥāq al-Hindī al-Ḥanafī (d. 773 AH) the author of *Sharḥ al-hidāya* and *Sharḥ al-'aynī*, Najm al-Dīn al-Bahī al-Ḥanbalī (d. 802 AH), al-Jabartī (d. 806 AH), the lexicographer al-Fayrūzābādī (d. 818 AH), Shams al-Dīn al-Bisāṭī al-Mālikī (d. 842 AH), al-Munāwī (d. 871 AH), and many others. Of note with regard to the above is the abundant use of Ibn 'Arabī's sayings by al-Munāwī in his commentary of al-Suyūṭī's *Jāmi' al-ṣaghīr* entitled *Fayḍ al-qadīr*, and by al-Fayrūzābādī in his commentary on al-Bukhārī's *Ṣaḥīḥ*.[19] Also of note is the fact that al-Biqā'ī himself was a Sufi and that he received the Sufi mantle or *khirqa* from his shaykh, 'Abd Allāh b. Khalīl al-Qal'ī al-Dimashqī al-Shāfi'ī![20]

When the same al-Biqā'ī attacked al-Ghazzālī for saying, "There is no possibility of anything more perfect than what exists,"[21] al-Suyūṭī again refuted al-Biqā'ī's insinuations in his epistle *Tashdīd al-arkān fī laysa fīl-imkān abda'u mimmā kān* [The buttressing of the pillars concerning al-Ghazzālī's saying "there is no possibility of anything more perfect than what exists"].[22] Imam al-Haytamī refers to the incident in his *Fatāwā ḥadīthiyya*:

> Al-Biqā'ī's fanaticism led him to criticize the saying of al-Ghazzālī, the Proof of Islam, "There is no possibility of anything more perfect than what exists." He went vituperating him until people became disgusted. Then, one day, he went to visit one of the scholars of knowledge who was sitting somewhere alone. The latter took his slipper and began to hit al-Biqā'ī with it until he almost destroyed it, all the while scolding him, saying: "Are you the one who criticizes al-Ghazzālī?! Are you the one who says such-and-such about him?!" until some people came and rescued him, although no one disapproved of the incident. Following this, the people of his time rallied against al-Biqā'ī and published many refutations against him in defense of al-Ghazzālī.

> The gist of their replies concerning al-Ghazzālī's statement is that when the Divine will linked itself to the origination of this world and He originated it, ordaining the abiding of part of it to a set limit and that of its remainder indefinitely—meaning paradise and hellfire—this precluded the linkage (*ta'alluq*) of Divine power to the eradication (*i'dām*) of the entirety of this world. For Divine power is not linked except to the possible, while the eradication of the entirety of this world is not possible—not ontologically (*li-dhātih*) but because of the aforementioned linkage. Since its eradication is excluded according to what we said, it follows that its origination in the first place was the apex of wisdom and completion, and the most perfect of all that can possibly be created, for, as concluded above, there is none other in existence.[23]

Al-Suyūṭī also marked his distate for al-Dhahabī's aspersions against early and late Sufi authorities and his anti-Ash'arī tone in many entries of his *Mīzān al-i'tidāl,* notably that of the early Sufi *mutakallim* al-Ḥārith al-Muḥāsibī, in which he quotes the aspersions of the hadith master Abū Zur'a then exclaims:

> And where are the likes of al-Ḥārith al-Muḥāsibī? How then if Abū Zur'a saw the books of later Sufis such as the *Qūt al-qulūb* of Abū Ṭālib [al-Makkī], and where are the likes of the *Qūt*? How then if he saw *Bahjat al-asrār* of Abū Jahḍam, and *Ḥaqā'iq al-tafsīr* of al-Sulamī, he would jump to the ceiling! How then if he saw the books of Abū Ḥāmid al-Ṭūsī [Imam al-Ghazzālī]. . . ? the *Ghunya* of Shaykh 'Abd al-Qādir [al-Jīlānī]. . . the *Fuṣūṣ al-ḥikam* and *Futūḥāt al-makiyya* [of Ibn 'Arabī]?![24]

Al-Suyūṭī responds strenuously to al-Dhahabī:

> Do not let al-Dhahabī's mumblings deceive you, for he went so far as to mumble against Imam Fakhr al-Dīn b. al-Khaṭīb [al-Rāzī] and against one who is greater than the Imam, namely, Abū Ṭālib al-Makkī the author of *Qūt al-qulūb*, and against one who is greater than Abū Ṭālib, namely, Shaykh Abū al-Ḥasan al-Ash'arī, whose fame has filled the firmaments! And al-Dhahabī's books are filled with that: *al-Mīzān*, *al-Tārīkh*, and *Siyar al-nubalā'*. Are you going to accept his words against their likes? Never, by God! His word is not accepted

concerning them. Rather, we respect their right over us and render it to them in full.[25]

His Ash'arism

Al-Suyūṭī was Ash'arī in doctrine as shown in many of his works. In *Masālik al-ḥunafā fī waliday al-muṣṭafā* [Methods of those with pure belief concerning the parents of the Prophet ﷺ] he says:

> The Prophet's ﷺ parents died before he was sent as Prophet and there is no punishment for them, since *We never punish until We send a messenger whom they reject* (Qur'an 17:15). Our Ash'arī imams among those in *kalām*, *uṣūl*, and *fiqh* agree on the statement that one who dies while *da'wa* has not reached him, dies saved. This has been defined by Imam al-Shāfi'ī [. . .] Some of the *fuqahā'* explained that the reason is, such a person follows *fitra* or pristine disposition, and has not stubbornly refused nor rejected any messenger.[26]

Of the narration from Abū Mūsā al-Ash'arī: "The *kursī* is the footstool and it groans like a new saddle"[27] al-Suyūṭī says in *al-Durr al-manthūr*: "This is a metaphor (*hādha 'alā sabīl al-isti'āra*). This [metaphorical] meaning is made clear by Ibn Jarīr's narration from al-Daḥḥāk whereby 'The *kursī* is placed below the throne and is where the angels stand.' "

Al-Suyūṭī's elucidation is confirmed by what al-Qurṭubī—another Ash'arī—quoted from Ibn 'Aṭiyya in his *Tafsīr* of the Verse of the Throne whereby the meaning was that the *kursī* was placed in front of the *'arsh* "just like" the footstool is placed in front of a high chair, indicating that it did not necessitate reference to an actual footstool but referred, for example, to a seat or station. Al-Bayhaqī—also an Ash'arī—states the same.[28]

Al-Suyūṭī wrote *Majāz al-fursān ilā majāz al-Qur'ān*, an abridgment of *al-Ishāra ilā al-ījāz fī ba'ḍ anwā' al-majāz* or *Majāz al-Qur'ān* [The metaphors of the Qur'an] by the great Ash'arī imam, Sulṭān al-'Ulamā' al-'Izz b. 'Abd al-Salām in which the latter stated: "When God is described by something which is inapplicable to Him literally (*bī ḥaqīqatihi*), He is described by it only metaphorically."

In his commentary on Ibn Mājah's *Sunan*, al-Suyūṭī gave a thoroughly Ash'arī commentary on the concept of Divine aboveness as it is mentioned in the following hadith from al-'Abbās b. 'Abd al-Muṭṭalib ﵁ who said: "I was in al-Baṭḥā' with a group of people together with the Prophet ﷺ when a cloud passed over him. He looked at it and said:

> "What do you call this?" They replied: "Clouds." He said: "And the rain-bearing clouds." "And the rain-bearing clouds." "And the highest clouds. "And the highest clouds." The Prophet ﷺ said: "What do you suppose is the distance that lies between the heaven and the earth?" They replied: "We do not know." He said: "Verily, there is between the two a distance of one, or two, or three and seventy years. And the heaven above that heaven lies at an identical distance." He went on to count seven heavens in this fashion. Then he said: "Above the seventh heaven there is an ocean. Between its surface and its bottom lies the same distance as between one heaven and the next. Above that ocean there are eight mountain goats. Between their hooves and their knees lies the same distance as between one heaven and the next. On top of their shoulders (*'alā ẓuhūrihinna*) rests the throne. From its bottom to its top lies the same distance as between one heaven and the next. *And God is above that* (*wa Allāhu fawqa dhālik*)."

Al-Suyūṭī comments:

> Al-Ṭībī (d. 743 AH) said: "What is meant by 'seventy' here is to express great quantity, not an exact number (*al-takthīr lā al-taḥdīd*), in the light of what came to us to the effect that between the heaven and the earth and between each heaven lies a distance of five hundred years' travel." The hadith master Ibn Ḥajar reconciled [the two counts] in that "five hundred" is in the perspective of slowness, while this is in the perspective of swiftness.[29]

His statement: "Eight mountain goats." They are angels in the image of mountain goats,[30] as God said: *And the angels will be on the sides thereof, and eight will uphold the throne of their Lord that day, above them* (Qur'an 69:17).

His statement: "And God Almighty is above that." Al-Ṭībī said: "The Prophet ﷺ meant to direct them away from lower-worldly matters to higher-worldly ones (*min al-sufliyyāt ilā al-'uluwiyyāt*), and make them reflect on the dominion of the heavens and the throne. Then they rise up to the knowledge of their Creator, and they reject idol-worship with loathing, ceasing to associate anything with God in worship. Therefore, he rose with them from the clouds, then the heavens, then the ocean, then the *aw'āl*, then the throne, up to the Owner of the Throne. This rising is in the sense of magnificence (*al-'aẓama*), not location (*al-makān*). For, verily, God is beyond taking the throne as His dwelling (*manzil*) and settlement (*mustaqarr*)! Rather, God is its Creator and He is transcendent beyond direction and place."[31]

Al-Suyūṭī succintly defined Qadarī doctrine as: "the claim that evil is created by human beings."[32]

His Fatwas in Defense of the Prophet's ﷺ Parents

Al-Suyūṭī authored several epistles to show that the Prophet's parents must not be counted as other than saved, among them *Masālik al-ḥunafā', al-Durūj al-munīfa, al-Ta'ẓīm wal-minna*, and others.[33]

His Fatwa on the Mawlid

In his fatwa, *Ḥusn al-maqṣid fī 'amal al-mawlid* [The excellent goal in the celebration of the Prophetic birth] in his compendium titled *al-Ḥāwī lil-fatāwā* al-Suyūṭī says:

> The reason for gathering for *tarāwīḥ* prayers is sunna and seeking nearness to God (*qurba*). Similarly, we say that the reason for gathering to celebrate the *mawlid* is recommended (*mandūb*) and an act of drawing near (*qurba*) and that the intention to celebrate the *mawlid* is excellent (*mustaḥsana*) without a doubt.

One of the reasons al-Suyūṭī wrote this fatwa was to refute point by point the objections of Shaykh Tāj al-Dīn 'Umar b. 'Alī al-Lakhmī al-Fākihānī (d. 734 AH) to the celebration of the *mawlid*. Shaykh Aḥmad Zarrūq said in his commentary on al-Qasṭallānī's *al-Mawāhib al-lāduniyya*: "As for the claim by al-Tāj al-Fākihānī, one of our Mālikī colleagues, that the celebration of the *mawlid* is a reprehensible and lowly innovation, al-Suyūṭī took care of refuting all that he forwarded in support of his claim word for word—may God grant him increased care and kindness!" Al-Kattānī cited it in *al-Yumnu wal-is'ād bi-mawlidi khayr al-'ibād*.[34]

His Fatwa on the Number of Tarāwīḥ Prayers

Al-Suyūṭī said: "Surely, if the exact number of the *tarāwīḥ* had been a subject of textual stipulation, it would have been impermissible to the first generations to add anything to it. The people of Madīna and the early Muslims were certainly more scrupulous than to commit such an act!"[35]

His Rank of Mujtahid Muṭlaq

Al-Suyūṭī was taken to task for his claim that he was capable of independent scholarly exertion or *ijtihād muṭlaq* in *al-Taḥadduth bi-ni'mat Allāh*:

> As for *ijtihād*, I have reached—praise belongs to God for His munificence—the rank of absolute *ijtihād* in legal rulings, in the Prophetic hadith, and in Arabic. The rank of *ijtihād* in those three spheres was gathered in the person of Shaykh Taqī al-Dīn al-Subkī and was never gathered in anyone after him except myself [. . .] In the time before al-Subkī, *ijtihād* in the rulings and in hadith was gathered in several people, among them Ibn Taymiyya, and before him Ibn Daqīq al-'Īd, and before him al-Nawawī, and before him Abū Shāma, and before him Ibn al-Ṣalāḥ. As for earlier authorities it is very abundant.[36]

In a later work he explains, somewhat apologetically: "I did not mean by that that I was similar to one of the four imams, but only that I was an affiliated *mujtahid* (*mujtahid muntasib*). For, when I reached the level of *tarjīḥ* or distinguishing the best fatwa inside the school, I did not contravene al-Nawawī's *tarjīḥ*. And when I reached the level of *ijtihād muṭlaq*, I did not contravene al-Shāfi'ī's school." He continued: "There is not in our time, on the face of the earth, from east to west, anyone more knowledgeable than myself in hadith and the Arabic language, save al-Khaḍir or the pole of saints or some other *walī*—none of whom I include in my statement—and God knows best."[37]

In *Ḥusn al-muḥāḍara* he states:

> I was granted profound expertise in seven sciences: exegesis, hadith [and its nomenclature], *fiqh*, grammar, philology, and rhetoric in the tradition of the Arabs and those of superlative eloquence—not that of the non-Arabs and the philosophers; and a level below the above level of those seven sciences in the principles of *fiqh*, dialectic, and declension, and below it yet in composition, epistolary style, and inheritance laws, and below it in the canonical readings which I did not take from any teacher, and below it in medicine. As for arithmetic it is the hardest thing for me and the remotest from my mind: whenever I look into a matter related to it, it is as if I try to carry a mountain [. . .] In my beginnings I had tried to read some logic but God cast its dislike into my heart and I heard that Ibn al-Ṣalāḥ had declared it illicit, so I abandoned it and God compensated me with the science of hadith, which is the noblest science [. . .] As for the first seven sciences, I do not think that any of my shaykhs reached my level in them except *fiqh*, for in that science my teacher was more proficient and expert than I.

Al-Suyūṭī includes Abū Muḥammad al-Juwaynī—the father of Imam al-Ḥaramayn—among the absolute *mujtahids*.[38]

His Rank of Mujaddid

In *Tuḥfat al-mujtahidīn bi-asmā' al-mujaddidīn* [The gem of the striving scholars: the names of the renewers of the religion] and *al-Taḥadduth bi-ni'mat Allāh* al-Suyūṭī listed the renewers as follows:

1st century: 'Umar b. 'Abd al-'Azīz;
2nd century: al-Shāfi'ī;
3rd century: Ibn Surayj and al-Ash'arī;
4th century: Ibn al-Bāqillānī, Sahl al-Ṣu'lūkī, Abū Ḥāmid al-Isfarāyīnī, and Abū Isḥāq al-Shīrāzī;
5th century: al-Ghazzālī and Abū Ṭāhir al-Silafī;
6th century: al-Fakhr al-Rāzī, al-Rāfi'ī, and al-Nawawī;
7th century: Ibn Daqīq al-'Īd (625–702 AH);[39]

8th century: al-Bulqīnī, al-'Irāqī, and Nāṣir al-Dīn b. bint al-Maylaq al-Shādhilī; and
9th century: al-Suyūṭī and Shaykh al-Islam al-Qāḍī Zakariyyā al-Anṣārī.

It is possible to add to the above mostly-Shāfi'ī list the following mostly-Ḥanafī authorities:

2nd century: Abū Ḥanīfa;
3rd century: al-Ṭaḥāwī and al-Māturīdī;
4th century: Abū Bakr al-Rāzī (al-Jaṣṣāṣ);
5th century: al-Sarakhsī;
6th century: al-Marghinānī;
7th century: al-Nasafī;
8th century: al-Maḥbūbī; Imam al-Lacknawī in *al-Fawā'id al-bahiyya* said this century saw the following peerless experts each in his field: al-Bulqīnī in Shāfi'ī *fiqh*, Zayn al-Dīn al-'Irāqī in hadith, Sirāj al-Dīn b. al-Mulaqqin in prolific works, Shams al-Dīn al-Fanārī in his proficiency in all the rational, historical, and lexical sciences, Muḥammad b. 'Arafa al-Waraghmī in Mālikī *fiqh* and all the Arabic sciences, and Majd al-Dīn al-Fayrūzābādī al-Shīrāzī in Arabic.
9th century: Kamāl b. al-Humām;
10th century: Ibn Nujaym.
11th century: al-Ḥaskafī and Shaykh Aḥmad al-Fārūqī of Sirhind (d. 1034);
12th century: al-Quṭb 'Abd Allāh al-Ḥaddād of Hadramawt, Yemen;
13th century: Shaykh Khālid al-Baghdādī and his student Shaykh Muḥammad Amīn 'Ābidīn (Ibn 'Ābidīn), both of Damascus; Shāh Walī Allāh and his son Shāh 'Abd al-'Azīz, both of Delhi; Imam Abū al-Ḥasanāt Muḥammad 'Abd al-Ḥay al-Lacknawī, Uthmān dān Fōdiō of Nigeria; and
14th century: Shaykh Badr al-Dīn al-Ḥasanī al-Maghribī of Damascus, Shaykh Muḥammad Zāhid al-Kawtharī of Turkey, Imam Aḥmad Riḍā Khān of India, and Shaykh Aḥmad b. Muṣṭafā al-Alawī of Algeria.

Al-ʻAẓīm Ābādī followed up al-Suyūṭī's list with the following differences:

1st century: Ibn Shihāb al-Zuhrī, al-Qāsim b. Muḥammad, Sālim b. ʻAbd Allāh, al-Ḥasan al-Baṣrī, Muḥammad b. Sīrīn, and Muḥammad al-Bāqir;
2nd century: Yaḥyā b. Maʻīn;
3rd century: al-Nasāʼī;
4th century: al-Ḥākim, ʻAbd al-Ghanī al-Maqdisī (d. 404 AH);
11th century: Ibrāhīm b. Ḥasan al-Kurdī al-Kawrānī al-Madanī;
12th century: Ṣāliḥ b. Muḥammad b. Nūḥ al-Fulānī al-Madanī, al-Sayyid Murtaḍā al-Zabīdī; and
13th century: Sayyid Nadhīr Ḥusayn, al-Qāḍī Ḥusayn b. Muḥammad al-Anṣārī al-Khazrajī al-Saʻdī al-Yamānī, Nawāb Ṣiddīq Ḥasan Khān Bhūpālī al-Qinnawjī.[40]

A Syrian author, ʻAdnān Kurdī, in his *Mujaddidūn fīl-Islām*, adds the following to al-Suyūṭī's list:

6th century: Ismāʻīl b. Muḥammad al-Taymī (d. 534 AH);
11th century: ʻAlī al-Qārī (d. 1014 AH);
12th century: Muḥammad b. ʻAbd al-Rasūl al-Barzanjī (d. 1113 AH); al-Mahdī and Jesus son of Maryam.

THE REMEMBRANCE OF GOD

The Outcome of Contemplation over Loud *Dhikr*

(*Natījatu al-fikr fīl-jahri bil-dhikr*)

By

IMAM JALĀL AL-DĪN AL-SUYŪṬĪ

بسم الله الرحمن الرحيم

All praise is due to God and it is enough! Salutations of peace upon His chosen servants! You have asked—may God honor you!—concerning the custom of the Sufi masters in setting up circles for the purpose of *dhikr* (remembrance) and reciting it aloud in the mosques raising the voice with *tahlīl* [saying *lā ilāha illā Allāh*]. You ask whether this is disapproved (*makrūh*) or not?

There is nothing disapproved in any of the above at all. In fact, many hadiths imply that loud *dhikr* is desirable (*mustaḥabb*) while other hadiths imply that silent *dhikr* is desirable. The two statements are reconciled in the fact that desirability varies in accordance with varying circumstances and individuals. This is how Imam al-Nawawī similarly reconciled the hadiths that prefer loud recitation of the Qur'an with those that prefer muted recitation. I shall explain this point section by section.

HADITHS WHICH EITHER EXPLICITLY OR IMPLICITLY PROVE THE DESIRABILITY OF LOUDNESS IN *DHIKR*

The First Hadith

Al-Bukhārī narrated from Abū Hurayra ﵁ that the Messenger of God ﷺ said:

> God the Almighty says, "I am as My servant thinks of Me, and I am with him when he remembers Me. If he mentions Me within himself I mention him within Myself. If he mentions Me in a gathering, I mention him in a better gathering."[1]

Dhikr performed in a gathering can only be done aloud.

The Second Hadith

Al-Bazzār and al-Ḥākim in the *Mustadrak*—the latter grading it sound (*ṣaḥīḥ*)—narrated from Jābir ﵁ that the Prophet ﷺ came out to us and said:

> "O people! God the Almighty has angelic troops that descend and join the gatherings of *dhikr* on earth. So go graze in the gardens of paradise!" They asked, "Where are the gardens of paradise?" He replied, "The gatherings of *dhikr*. So take part in the remembrance of God the Almighty morning and evening."[2]

The Third Hadith

Muslim and al-Ḥākim—this is his wording—narrated from Abū Hurayra ؓ that the Messenger of God ﷺ said:

> God the Almighty has worthy angels wander in search of the gatherings of *dhikr* on earth. When they find a *dhikr* gathering, they close in against one another's wings all the way to the heaven. God the Almighty then says, "From whence have you come?" They reply, "We have come from [a group of] Your servants who are exalting You, magnifying You, praising You, declaring Your Oneness, supplicating You, and seeking Your protection." God the Almighty asks, though He knows best, "And what do they ask?" They answer, "They ask you for paradise." He says, "Why, have they seen it?" They reply, "Our Lord, no!" God the Almighty says, "What if they had seen it!" Then He asks, "From what do they seek My protection?" Yet He knows about them better than anyone. They reply, "From the fire." He asks, "And have they seen it?" They say, "No." He continues, "What if they had seen it!" Then He says, "Bear witness that I have forgiven them and granted them what they request from Me and given them protection against that from which they sought my protection." Then the angels say, "Our Lord! There is among them a very sinful person who just happened to sit with them but is not one of them." To this God the Almighty replies, "Him also I have forgiven! They are such people as none sits with them and then perishes."[3]

The Fourth Hadith

Muslim and al-Tirmidhī narrated from both Abū Hurayra and Abū Saʿīd al-Khudrī ؓ that the Messenger of God ﷺ said:

> No group of people mention God the Almighty except the angels surround them closely, mercy envelops them, tranquility descends upon them, and God the Almighty mentions them among those that are with Him.[4]

The Fifth Hadith

Muslim and al-Tirmidhī narrated from Muʿāwiya that the Prophet came out and found some of his companions [sitting] in a circle. He asked:

> "What made you sit?" They replied: "We are sitting remembering God the Almighty and praising Him." He said: "Gabriel came to me and informed me that God the Almighty is vaunting you before the angels!"[5]

The Sixth Hadith

Al-Ḥākim—he graded it sound (*saḥīḥ*)—and al-Bayhaqī in *Shuʿab al-īmān* narrated that Abū Saʿīd al-Khudrī said that the Messenger of God said:

> Mention God the Almighty abundantly until they call you mad.[6]

The Seventh Hadith

Al-Bayhaqī narrated in *Shuʿab al-īmān* from [the *tābiʿī*] Abū al-Jawzā' that the Messenger of God said:

> Perform the *dhikr* of God the Almighty so much that the hypocrites say to you, "You are doing this for show."[7]

This is a *mursal* hadith [missing the companion-link]. The proof in this hadith and the one before it is in the fact that they [the hypocrites] will only say this when they hear *dhikr* done out loud, not silently.

The Eighth Hadith

Al-Bayhaqī narrated from Anas that the Messenger of God said:

> "When you pass by the gardens of paradise, graze well from them." They asked: "Messenger of God, what are the gardens of paradise?" He replied: "The circles of *dhikr*."[8]

The Ninth Hadith

Baqī b. Makhlad narrates from ʿAbd Allāh b. ʿAmr ؓ:

> The Prophet ﷺ passed by two gatherings, the first were supplicating God the Almighty and longing for Him, while the latter were teaching knowledge. He said ﷺ "Both are full of goodness and one is better than the other."[9]

The Tenth Hadith

Al-Bayhaqī narrated from ʿAbd Allāh b. Mughaffal ؓ that the Messenger of God ﷺ said:

> No people gather together to remember God except a caller from the heaven calls out to them: "Rise forgiven! I have changed your bad deeds into good deeds."[10]

The Eleventh Hadith

Al-Bayhaqī narrated from Abū Saʿīd al-Khudrī ؓ that the Messenger of God ﷺ said:

> The Lord Supreme shall say on the day of resurrection: "Today, the great multitude shall know who the beneficiaries of munificence are!" Someone asked, "Who are the beneficiaries of munificence, Messenger of God?" He replied: "The gatherings of *dhikr* in the mosques."[11]

The Twelfth Hadith

Al-Bayhaqī narrated that Ibn Masʿūd ؓ said:

> Truly, mountains call out to one another by their names, saying: "O So-and-so, has any rememberer of God the Almighty passed by you today?" If it replies "Yes," the other is pleased. Then ʿAbd Allāh [ibn Masʿūd] recited: *Indeed ye have put forth a thing most monstrous! At it the skies are about to burst, the earth to split asunder, and the mountains to fall down in utter ruin, that they attributed a son to the Most Gracious* (Qur'an 19:89–91). Then he said: "Do they hear falsehoods and not hear the good?"[12]

The Thirteenth Hadith

Ibn Jarīr [al-Ṭabarī] narrated in his *Tafsīr* that Ibn ʿAbbās رضي الله عنهما said in explanation of the verse *And neither heaven nor earth shed a tear over them*[13] (Qur'an 44:29):

> Truly, when a believer dies, that spot of earth upon which he used to pray and remember God the Almighty mourns him.[14]

Ibn Abī al-Dunyā narrates that Abū ʿUbayd said:

> Truly, when a believer dies, the regions of the earth cry out: "The believing servant of God has died!" Thereupon both the earth and the heaven begin to weep. The Most Merciful asks: "Why do you weep for My servant?" They reply: "Our Lord! He never trod anywhere in our parts except he remembered You."[15]

The proof in all of the above is in the fact that the hearing of the mountains and the earth for the *dhikr* can only take place when *dhikr* is done out loud.

The Fourteenth Hadith

Al-Bazzār and al-Bayhaqī narrate with a sound transmission chain from Ibn ʿAbbās رضي الله عنهما that the Messenger of God ﷺ said that God the Almighty said:

> My servant, whenever you remember Me in seclusion I remember you in seclusion; and whenever you mention Me in a gathering I mention you in a better gathering and a greater one![16]

The Fifteenth Hadith

Al-Bayhaqī narrated from Zayd b. Aslam that Ibn al-Adraʿ رضي الله عنه said:

> I went with the Messenger of God ﷺ one night, and he passed by a man in the mosque who was raising his voice. I said, "Messenger of God, perhaps he is doing this for show?" He replied, "No, rather, he is an enraptured supplicant (*lā wa-lākinnahu awwāh*)."[17]

Al-Bayhaqī also narrated from ʻUqba b. Āmir ؓ:

> The Messenger of God ﷺ said of a man known as Dhūl-Bijādayn[18] that he made plaintive cries (*innahu awwāh*) and this is because he was remembering God the Almighty.[19]

Al-Bayhaqī further narrates from Jābir b. ʻAbd Allāh ؓ:

> A man used to raise his voice with the remembrance of God the Almighty, whereupon someone said: "If only this man lowered his voice!" The Messenger of God ﷺ said: "Leave him, for he makes rapturous exclamations (*fa-innahu awwāh*)."[20]

The Sixteenth Hadith

Al-Ḥākim narrated from Shaddād b. Aws ؓ:

> We were in the presence of the Messenger of God ﷺ when he suddenly said: "Raise your hands and say: *lā ilāha illā Allāh!*" We did this. The Messenger of God ﷺ then said: "O God our Lord, You have indeed sent me with this blessed word (*kalima*) and commanded me to say it and promised me paradise on account of it. Truly, You never take back Your promise!" Then he said, "Be glad, God has forgiven you!"[21]

The Seventeenth Hadith

Al-Bazzār narrated from Anas ؓ that the Messenger of God ﷺ said:

> God the Almighty has wandering groups of angels who search out sessions of *dhikr*. When they find such gatherings, they surround them closely. God the Almighty commands them: "Cover them completely with My mercy! For they are such people as none sits with them and then perishes."[22]

The Eighteenth Hadith

Al-Ṭabarānī and Ibn Jarīr narrate from ʿAbd al-Raḥmān b. Sahl b. Ḥunayf ﷺ:

> The following verse was revealed to the Messenger of God ﷺ when he was in his quarters: *And keep yourself content with those who call on their Lord morning and evening* (Qur'an 18:28), whereupon he came out in search of these people. He found a group of them who were busy in the remembrance of God the Almighty. Among these people were those with disheveled hair and desiccated skin wearing only single garments. When he saw them he sat with them and said: "Praise be to God the Almighty who made such people among my *umma* and commanded me to keep myself content with them!"[23]

The Nineteenth Hadith

Imam Aḥmad narrated in *al-Zuhd* from Thābit:

> Salman al-Fārisī ﷺ was with a group of people that were engaged in the remembrance of God the Almighty when the Messenger of God ﷺ passed by them and they stopped. He asked: "What were you saying?" They replied: "We were mentioning God the Almighty." He said: "I saw mercy descending upon you and loved to take part in it with you!" Then he said: "Praise be to God the Almighty who made such people among my *umma* and commanded me to keep myself content with them!"[24]

The Twentieth Hadith

Al-Aṣbahānī reports in the *Targhīb*[25] from Abū Razīn al-ʿUqaylī [Laqīṭ b. Ṣabira] ﷺ that the Messenger of God ﷺ said to him: "Shall I not inform you of the mainstay of this whole affair by which you will achieve the best of this world and the next?" He replied: "Yes—please do!" The Messenger of God ﷺ said: "Keep to the gatherings of *dhikr* and, when you are alone, [even then] keep your tongue moving with the *dhikr* of God."[26]

The Twenty-first Hadith

Ibn Abī al-Dunyā, al-Bayhaqī, and al-Aṣbahānī narrated from Anas that the Messenger of God ﷺ said:

> That I sit with a people who remember God the Almighty after the morning prayer until the sun rises is dearer to me than the whole world over which the sun rises! Likewise, that I sit with a people who remember God the Almighty after the mid-afternoon prayer until the sun sets is dearer to me than the world and all it contains.[27]

The Twenty-second Hadith

The two arch-masters [al-Bukhārī and Muslim] narrated from Ibn 'Abbas: "The people raised their voices in *dhikr* when they finished their obligatory prayers in the time of the Messenger of God ﷺ." Ibn 'Abbas said: "By hearing this [*dhikr*] I would know when they had just completed their prayers."[28]

The Twenty-third Hadith

Al-Ḥākim narrated from 'Umar b. al-Khaṭṭāb that the Messenger of God ﷺ said:

> Whoever enters the marketplace and says: "There is no God but God alone, no partner does He have, His is the kingdom and His is the glory, He gives life and He gives death, and He is all-powerful over all things" (*Lā ilāha illā Allāhu waḥdahu lā sharīka lahu lahul mulku wa-lahul ḥamdu yuḥyī wa-yumītu wa-huwa 'alā kulli shay'in qadīr*), God the Almighty shall record for him one million good deeds, erase one million of his sins, raise his rank one million times, and a house is built for him in paradise." Some reports have: "[Whoever enters the marketplace] and calls out."[29]

The Twenty-fourth Hadith

Aḥmad, Abū Dāwūd, al-Tirmidhī—he declared it *ṣaḥīḥ*, al-Nasā'ī, and Ibn Mājah narrated from al-Sā'ib that the Messenger of God ﷺ

said: "Gabriel came to me and said, 'Order your companions to raise their voices in saying *Allāhu akbar!*' "[30]

The Twenty-fifth Hadith

Al-Marwazī narrated in *Kitāb al-'īdayn* from Mujāhid that 'Abd Allāh b. 'Umar and Abū Hurayra ﷺ would enter the marketplace in the ten [first] days [of *Dhūl Ḥijjah*] raising their voices in *takbīr* (saying: *Allāhu akbar*) and they did not go there for any other reason.[31]

He also narrated from 'Ubayd b. 'Umayr: " 'Umar ﷺ used to raise the *takbīr* in his tent. Then the people in the mosques would raise *takbīr* followed by the people in the markelace until the whole of Minā shook with *takbīr*."[32]

He also narrated from Maymūn b. Mahrān: "I found that the people raised *takbīr* in the ten [first] days of Dhūl Ḥijjah so much that it resembled the waves of the sea because of its abundance."

CONCLUSION

If you consider carefully the hadiths we adduced above you will realize from their collective evidence that there is no offensiveness whatsoever in loud *dhikr*. Rather, they contain evidence that it is desirable (*mustaḥabb*), some of these hadith being explicit while others are implicit, as we have indicated.

As for countering it [the desirability of loud *dhikr*] with the hadith: "The best *dhikr* is the silent one" (*khayr al-dhikr al-khafī*):[33] it is like arguing against the hadiths on loud recitation of the Qur'an on the basis of the hadith "The one who recites Qur'an silently is like the one who gives *ṣadaqa* in secret" (*al-musirru bil-Qur'ān kal-musirri bil-ṣadaqa*).[34]

Imam al-Nawawī reconciled the above in that silent *dhikr* is better when there is fear of show or when it would disturb those praying or those who are asleep, while loud *dhikr* is better in all other cases because it entails more work, its benefit involves the listeners, it awakens the reciter's heart, musters his energy toward reflection, focuses his hearing toward it, banishes drowsiness, and refreshes vigor.[35]

According to some it is desirable (*mustaḥabb*) to have part of one's recitation out loud and part of it silently. The silent reciter might get restless, so loud recitation cheers him up, while the loud reciter might get tired, so reciting silently will relax him.[36]

We say that the selfsame distinctions hold true for *dhikr*, and thus the various hadiths can be reconciled.[37]

If you were to argue producing the following verse: *And do you bring your Lord to remembrance in your very soul, with humility, and remember without loudness in words* (Qur'an 7:205), then let me tell you that this verse has three dimensions.[38]

The First Dimension

This verse was revealed in Makka as was the verse of al-Isrā': *Neither speak your prayer aloud, nor speak it in a low tone, but seek a middle course between* (Qur'an 17:110), at a time when the Messenger of God ﷺ recited the Qur'an aloud, whereupon the idolators would hear him and hurl abuse at the Qur'an and at God the Almighty who sent it. So He ordered to leave loud recitation as a preventive measure just as He also forbade the believers from hurling abuse at their idols in the following verse: *Do not revile those whom they call upon besides God, lest they out of spite revile God in their ignorance* (Qur'an 6:108).

Later on, this objective came to an end as conditions improved. This is indicated by Ibn Kathīr in his *Tafsīr*, where he states that the purpose of the above verse (Qur'an 6:108) is the same as for the previous verse: *Neither speak your prayer aloud nor speak it in a low tone but seek a middle course between* (Qur'an 17:110): whenever the idolators heard the Qur'an being recited they hurled abuse at it, at God the Almighty and His Messenger, so God the Almighty commanded the Messenger to lower his voice in recitation such that idolators would not hear, not too silently so that the companions could not make out what was being said, but to adopt a middle way between the two.[39]

The Second Dimension

A group of exegetes including 'Abd al-Raḥmān b. Zayd b. Aslam—Mālik's teacher—and Ibn Jarīr [al-Ṭabarī] understood this verse to refer to someone making *dhikr* while the Qur'an is being recited. That is, one is ordered to make *dhikr* in such fashion as a mark of respect for the book of God the Almighty with which voices should be raised. This view is reinforced by its connection with the [previous] verse: *When the Qur'an is recited, listen to it with attention and hold your peace that you may receive mercy* (Qur'an 7:204).

It may be that the command to be quiet caused concern that it might lead to apathy, hence [God] warned that even if they are commanded to keep silent with the tongue, nevertheless, the legal obligation of *dhikr* with the heart remains, so that one not neglect the *dhikr* of God altogether. This is why the verse ends with: *And do not be of those who are unheedful* (Qur'an 7:205).

The Third Dimension

The Sufis have mentioned that the command in this verse is specific to the Prophet ﷺ, the perfect and perfected exemplar. As for ordinary folk who are prone to whisperings and whims, they have been commanded to recite aloud because it is a more effective way of repelling such thoughts.

This view is supported by the hadith narrated by al-Bazzār from Mu'ādh b. Jabal ؓ that the Messenger of God ﷺ said:

> Whoever of you prays [supererogatory prayers] at night, let him raise his voice in his recitation, for truly the angels pray along with him and listen attentively to his recitation, and any of the believing jinn who happen to be in the air around him or who neighbor him in his dwelling also join him in his prayer and listen attentively to his recitation. Truly, because of his reciting aloud, all the corru ones among the jinn and the rebellious devils are expelled from his home and neighborhood.[40]

If you were to argue that God the Almighty said: *Call on your Lord with humility and in private: for God loves not those who trespass beyond bounds* (Qur'an 7:55) and that the exceeding of bounds here was explained to refer to loudness in supplication,[41] there are two sides to the answer:

First, the preponderant explication of this verse is that it refers to the supplication in which the original command is exceeded by the one supplicating, or the invention of a supplication that has no basis in the law.[42] This interpretation is supported by the report narrated by Ibn Mājah and al-Ḥākim his *Mustadrak*—he declared it sound—from Abū Nu'āma:

> 'Abd Allāh b. Mughaffal heard his son praying: "O God the Almighty! I ask You for the white palace on the right side of paradise." pon hearing this he said [to his son]: "I have heard the Messenger of God ﷺ saying: 'There will come a time when some people in my *umma* who will trespass bounds in their supplication.' "[43]

This is the explication of a companion, and he knew better [than we] as to its meaning.

Second, supposing the objection was granted, the verse refers to supplication and not to *dhikr*. A *du'ā'* in itself is better said secretly because this makes it likelier to be accepted. Hence God the Almighty said [in reference to Zakariyyā]: *Behold! he cried to his Lord in secret* (Qur'an 19:3). For this reason it is agreed upon that it is desirable (*mustaḥabb*) to make *isti'ādha* (seeking of protection) at the start of prayer secretly, because it happens to be a supplication.[44]

If you were to argue that it is narrated from 'Abd Allāh b. Mas'ūd that he saw some people saying *lā ilāha illā Allāh* raising their voices in the mosque, whereupon he said to them: "I do not think you are anything but innovators" and he expelled them from the mosque,[45] I say: this companion-report from Ibn Mas'ūd needs its chain of transmission thoroughly examined; and who among the imams of hadith mastership has narrated it in his book? And even supposing it were to be established as authentic, it would still be contradicting too many established hadiths which we have mentioned already, and in such a scenario such hadiths take priority.

In addition, I saw something which shows that the above was never the position of Ibn Mas'ūd: Imam Aḥmad b. Ḥanbal said in *Kitāb al-zuhd*:

> Ḥusayn b. Muḥammad narrated to us: al-Mas'ūdī[46] narrated to us from 'Āmir b. Shaqīq,[47] from Abū Wā'il: "Those people who claim that 'Abd Allāh [Ibn Mas'ūd] forbade *dhikr*! I never sat in any gathering with 'Abd Allāh exce he made *dhikr* of God in it."[48]

Imam Aḥmad also narrated in *al-Zuhd* from Thābit al-Bunānī: "I swear by God that those who remember God the Almighty (*ahl al-dhikr*) sit for the *dhikr* of God with sins comparable to mountains, but when they get up and leave having done *dhikr* of God, not a single sin remains on them."

Here ends the text of al-Suyūṭī's epistle,
Natījat al-fikr fīl-jahri bil-dhikr,
God have mercy on him
and reward
him!

APPENDIX I

PUBLISHED WORKS OF AL-SUYŪṬĪ

Below are the titles of some of al-Suyūṭī's works in print kept in the Arabic collection of the University of Princeton (New Jersey, USA) as of the year 1999. The most recent date has been given for works with more than one edition:

1. *Abwāb al-sa'āda fī asbāb al-shahāda* (1987) [The gates of felicity in the causes of the witnessing to oneness]
2. *al-Aḥādīth al-ḥisān fī faḍl al-ṭaylasān* (1983) [The fair narrations on the merit of the unstitched headshawl]
3. *Akhlāq ḥamalat al-Qur'ān* (1987) [Manners of the carriers of Qur'an]
4. *Alfiyyat al-Suyūṭī fī muṣṭalaḥ al-ḥadīth* (1988) [The thousand-line poem on hadith nomenclature]
5. *Alfiyyat al-Suyūṭī al-naḥwiyya* (1900) [The thousand-line poem on grammar]
6. *'Amal al-yawm wal-layla* (1987) [Supererogatory devotions for each day and night]
7. *Anīs al-jalīs* (1874) [The familiar companion]
8. *al-'Araj fīl-faraj* (1988) [A commentary on Ibn Abī al-Dunyā's "The deliverance," a work on hope and joy)
9. *al-Arba'ūn ḥadīth fī qawa'id al-aḥkām al-shar'iyya* (1986) [Forty narrations on basic legal rulings]
10. *Asbāb al-nuzūl* (1983) [Causes of Qur'anic revelation verse by verse]
11. *Asbāb wurūd al-ḥadīth* (1988) [Causes and circumstances of hadith]
12. *al-Ashbāh wal-naẓā'ir fī furū' al-Shāfi'iyya* [Interrelated topics in Shāfi'ī law]

13. *al-Ashbāh wal-naẓā'ir fīl-'Arabiyya* [Interrelated topics in Arabic]
14. *Asrār tartīb al-Qur'ān* (1976) [The secret in the ordering of the Qur'an]
15. *al-Āyat al-kubrā fī sharḥ qiṣṣat al-isra'* (1985) [The great sign: commentary on the story of the Prophet's night journey]
16. *'Ayn al-iṣāba fī istidrāk 'Ā'ishata 'alā al-ṣaḥāba* (1988) [Exactitude itself in 'Ā'isha's rectification of the companions]
17. *al-Azhār al-mutanāthira fīl-aḥādīth al-mutawātira* (1951) [The most prominent of the reports concerning the narrations of mass transmission]
18. *Badhl al-himma fī ṭalab barā'at al-dhimma* [Directing one's energies to pursue clearness of conscience]; contained in the collective volume entitled: *Thalāth rasā'il fīl-ghība* (1988) [Three epistles on slander]
19. *al-Bāhir fī ḥukm al-nabī* ﷺ *fīl-bāṭin wal-ẓāhir* (1987) [The dazzling light concerning the Prophet's judgment in hidden and visible matters]
20. *al-Bahjat al-marḍiyya fī sharḥ al-alfiyya* (1980) [The pleasing beauty: commentary on (Muḥammad b. 'Abd Allāh b. Mālik's) *Alfiyya*]
21. *Bulbul al-rawḍa* (1981) [Chronicle on al-rawḍa (Egypt)]
22. *Bushrā al-ka'īb bi liqā' al-ḥabīb* (1960) [The consolation of the sad with the meeting of the beloved]
23. *Daqāi'q al-akhbār fī dhikr al-jannati wal-nār* (1961) [The subtleties in the reports that mention paradise and the fire]
24. *al-Dībāj alā Ṣaḥīḥ Muslim b. al-Ḥajjāj* (1991) [Two-volume commentary on *Ṣaḥīḥ Muslim*]
25. *al-Durar al-muntathira fīl-aḥādīth al-mushtahara* (1988) [The scattered pearls of the famous narrations]; also published as *al-Nawāfiḥ al-'aṭira fīl-aḥādīth al-mushtahara* (1992) [The fragrant scents of the famous narrations]
26. *al-Durr al-manthūr fīl-tafsīr bi al-ma'thur* [The scattered pearls: a commentary of Qur'an based on transmitted reports]
27. *Durr al-saḥāba fīman dakhala Miṣr min al-ṣaḥāba* [Those of the companions that entered Egypt]; documenting 350 names, seven of them women.
28. *al-Durūj al-munīfa fīl-ābā' al-sharīfa* (1916) [The outstanding entries concerning the Prophet's ancestors]

29. *Faḍḍ al-wiʿāʾ fī aḥādīth rafʿ al-yadayn fīl-duʿā* (1985) [The emptying of the vessel concerning raising the hands when making supplication]
30. *al-Fawz al-ʿaẓīm fī liqāʾ al-karīm* (1994) [The great victory in meeting the all-generous]
31. *al-Ghurar fī faḍāʾil ʿUmar* (1991) [The radiant highlights: 'Umar's merits]
32. *al-Ḥabāʾik fī akhbār al-malāʾik* (1985) [The celestial orbits or the reports concerning the angels]
33. *Ḥaqīqat al-sunna wal-bidʿa* aw *al-Amr bil-ittibāʿ wal-nahī ʿan al-munkar* (1985) [The reality of sunna and innovation, or, The ordering of obedient following and the prohibition of evil-doing]
34. *al-Ḥāwī lil-fatāwī fīl-fiqh wa-ʿulūm al-tafsīr wal-ḥadīth wal-uṣūl wal-naḥwi wal-iʿrāb wa-sāʾir al-funūn* (1933) [The collected legal responses in jurisprudence, Qur'anic commentary, hadith, principles, language, and other sciences]
35. *al-Hayʾatu al-saniyya fīl-hayʾati al-sunniyya* (1982) [Treatise on astronomy]
36. *al-Ḥujaj al-mubayyana fīl-tafḍīl bayna Makkata wal-Madīna* (1985) [The proofs made manifest concerning the superexcellence of Makka and Madīna]
37. *Ḥusn al-maqṣid fī ʿamal al-mawlid* (1985) [Excellence of purpose in celebrating the birth of the Prophet ﷺ], also in the *Ḥāwī*
38. Ḥ*usn al-samti fīl-ṣamt* (1985) [The merits of silence]
39. *Iḥyāʾ al-mayt bi faḍāʾil ahl al-bayt* (1988) [Giving life to the dead, or, The merits of the family of the Prophet ﷺ]
40. *Ikhtilāf al-madhāhib* (1989) [The divergences among the schools of law]
41. *al-Iklīl fī istinbāṭ al-tanzīl* (1981) [The diadem: the extraction of rulings from the revealed book]
42. *Inbāh al-adhkiyāʾ fī ḥayāt al-anbiyāʾ* (1916) [Notice to the wise concerning the life of the prophets (i.e. in the grave)]
43. *al-Iqtirāḥ fī ʿilm uṣūl al-naḥw* (1978) [The authoritative discourse concerning the science of philology]
44. *Isbāl al-kisāʾ alā al-nisā* (1984) [Women and the donning of cover]
45. *al-Itqān fī ʿulūm al-Qurʾān* (1996) [Precision and mastery in the sciences of the Qur'an]

46. *al-Itḥāf bi-ḥubb al-ashrāf* (1900) [The present concerning love of the descendants of the Prophet ﷺ]
47. *al-Izdihār fīmā ʿaqadahu al-shuʿarāʾ min al-aḥādīth wal-āthār (1991)* [The flourishes of poets related to the prophetic narrations and sayings of the companions]
48. *Jamʿ al-jawāmiʿ, al-maʿrūf bil-jāmiʿ al-kabīr (1970)* [The collection of collections, known as the major collection]
49. *Jāmiʿ al-aḥādīth al-jāmiʿ al-ṣaghīr wa-zawāʾidihi* (1994) [The minor collection and its addenda]
50. *Janī al-jinās* (1986) [The genera of rhetoric]
51. *Jazīl al-mawāhib fī ikhtilāf al-madhāhib* (1992) [The abundant gifts concerning the differences among the schools of law]
52. *al-Kanz al-madfūn wal-falak al-mashḥūn* (1992) [The buried treasure in the laden ship (an encyclopedia of Islamic history)]
53. *Kashf al-ṣalṣala ʿan waṣf al-zalzala* (1987) [The transmitted expositions concerning the description of earthquakes]
54. *Kitāb asmāʾ al-mudallisīn* (1992) [The book of the names of narrators who conceal information]
55. *Kitāb bughyat al-wuʿāt fī ṭabaqāt al-lughawiyyīn* (1908) [The goal of the sagacious concerning the synchronical layers of lexicologists and philologists]
56. *Kitāb hamʿ al-hawāmiʿ sharḥ jamʿ al-jawāmiʿ fī ʿilm al-naḥw* (1973) [The rushing floodgates, or Commentary on the collection of collections on the science of grammar]
57. *Kitāb ḥusn al-muḥāḍara fī akhbāri Miṣra wal-Qāhira* (1904) [The excellent lectures concerning the chronicle of Egypt and Cairo]
58. *Kitāb itmām al-dirāya li qurrāʾ al-nuqāya* (1891) [The perfection of knowledge for the readers of [al-Suyūṭī's] *al-Nuqāya*]
59. *Kitāb lubb al-lubāb fī taḥrīr al-ansāb* (1840) [The kernel of kernels concerning the editorship of genealogies]
60. *Kitāb al-shamārikh fī ʿilm al-tārikh* (1894) [The book of date-heavy stalks: a primer on historiography]
61. *Kitāb al-shihāb al-thāqib fī dhamm al-khalīl* (1992) [The piercing arrows—a commentary (on the vizier and jurist ʿAlī b. Ẓāfir's "The healing of the parched concerning the castigation of one's dear friend,") on the ethics of friendship]

62. *Kitāb al-tabarrī min ma'arrat al-Ma'arrī wa-tuḥfat al-ẓurafā' bi-asmā' al-khulafā'* (1989) [Poetry on the names of the caliphs]
63. *Kitāb al-tadhkīr bil-marji' wal-maṣīr* (1991) [Book of the reminder of the return (to Allah)]
64. *Kitāb tuḥfat al-mujālis wa-nuzhat al-majālis* (1908) [The jewel of every fellow student and the pleasant gatherings]
65. *al-La'āli' al-maṣnū'a fīl-aḥādīth al-mawḍū'a* (1960) [The artificial pearls in the forged hadiths]
66. *Laqaṭ al-marjān fī aḥkām al-jānn* (1989) [The gleanings of coral: rulings concerning the jinn]
67. *Lubāb al-nuqūl fī asbāb al-nuzūl* (1981) [The best of narrations concerning the exact circumstances of revelation]
68. *al-Luma' fī khaṣā'iṣi yawmi al-jumu'a* (1986) [Virtues of the day of *jumu'a*]
69. *Mā rawāhu al-asāṭīn fī 'adam al-majī' ilā al-salāṭīn* (1992) [The reports on avoidance of the courts of rulers]; with *Dhamm al-maks* [Blame of taxes and tolls]
70. *Manāhil al-ṣafā fī takhrīj aḥādīth al-shifā* (1988) [The springs of purity: documentation of the hadiths mentioned in Qadi 'Iyāḍ's "The healing"]
71. *Manāqib al-khulafā' al-rāshidīn* (1890) [Virtues of the well-guided caliphs]
72. *al-Manhaj al-sawī wal-manhal al-rawī fīl-ṭibb al-nabawī* (1986) [The straight path and quenching spring in the Prophet's medicine]
73. *al-Maqāmāt al-sundusiyya fīl-nisbat al-muṣṭafawiyya* (1916) [The resplendent stations concerning the prophetic lineage]
74. *al-Maṣābīḥ fī ṣalāt al-tarāwīḥ* (1955) [The lanterns: on the prayer of rests (*tarāwīḥ*)]
75. *Masālik al-ḥunafā' fī wāliday al-muṣṭafā* (1993) [Method of those of pure religion concerning the parents of the Prophet ﷺ]
76. *al-Maṭāli' al-sā'ida sharḥ al-Suyūṭī 'alā al-alfiyya al-musammāt bi al-farīda fīl-naḥw wal-taṣrīf wal-khaṭṭ* (1981) [al-Suyūṭī's commentary on his own thousand-line poem entitled "The unique pearl" on philology, conjugation, and calligraphy]
77. *Maṭla' al-badrayn fīman yu'ṭā ajrahu marratayn* (1991) [The rising of the two full moons: those rewarded twice (i.e., sincere Christians who accept Islam)]

78. *Miftāḥ al-janna fīl-i'tiṣām bil-sunna* (1993) [The key to paradise which consists in clinging to the sunna of the Prophet ﷺ]
79. *Mufḥimāt al-aqrān fī mubhamāt al-Qur'ān* (1991) [The elucidations of the peers in the obscurities of the Qur'an]
80. *al-Muhadhdhab fīmā waqa'a fīl-Qur'ān min al-mu'arrab* (1988) [The emendation concerning the foreign words and phrases in the Qur'an]
81. *Mu'jiza ma'a karāma fī kitāb al-sharaf al-muḥattam: fīmā manna Allāhu ta'alā bihi 'alā waliyyihi Aḥmad al-Rifā'ī* (1965) [The evidentiary miracle and gift concerning the book of "The Paramount Honor" (by al-Rifā'ī) and what Allah has bestowed in it upon His friend Aḥmad (b. 'Alī) al-Rifā'ī]
82. *Mukhtaṣar sharḥ al-jāmi' al-saghīr lil-munāwī* (1954) [The abridged commentary of al-Suyūṭī's minor collection (by al-Munāwī)]
83. *Muntahā al-'amal fī sharḥ ḥadīth innamā al-a'māl* (1986) [The goal of all practice: commentary on the hadith actions count only according to intentions]
84. *Musnad Fāṭimat al-zahrā'* ؓ *wamā warada fī faḍliha* (1994) [Narrations traced back to Fāṭima the radiant and reports concerning her virtues]
85. *al-Mustaẓraf min akhbār al-jawārī* (1989) [The graceful reports concerning women slaves]
86. *Mutawakkilī fīmā warada fīl-Qur'āni bi al-lughat al-ḥabashiyya wal-fārisiyya wal-rūmiyya wal-hindiyya wal-siryāniyya wal-'ibrāniyya wal-nabaṭiyya wal-qibṭiyya wal-turkiyya wal-zanjiyya wal-barbariyya* [My reliance concerning words in the Qur'an in the Ethiopian, Farsi, Greek, Hindī, Syriac, Hebrew, Nabatean, Coptic, Turkic, African, and Berber tongues]
87. *Nashr al-'ilmayn al-munīfayn fī iḥyā' al-abawayn al-sharīfayn* (1916) [The proclamation to the two lofty knowledges (Qur'an and Sunna) concerning the resuscitation of the Prophet's parents (at his hands)]
88. *Natījat al-fikr fīl-jahri bil-dhikr* (1950) [The conclusion of reflection upon loud remembrance of Allah (translated in this edition as "The remembrance of God: the outcome of contemplation over loud dhikr")]

89. *Naẓm al-iqyān fī a'yān al-a'yān* (1927) [Who's who in the ninth hijri century]
90. *al-Nukāt al-badī'a 'alā al-mawḍū'āt* (1991) [al-Suyūṭī's critique of Ibn al-Jawzī's collection of forged narrations]
91. *Nuzhat al-julasā' fī ashhari al-nisā'* (1986) [The recreation of (student) gatherings concerning famous women (poets)]
92. *Nuzhat al-muta'ammil wa-murshid al-muta'ahhil fīl-khaṭīb wal-mutazawwij* (1989) [The recreation of the fiancé and the guide of the married]
93. *Nuzhat al-'umr fīl-tafḍīl bayna al-bīḍ wal-sumr* (1931) [The recreation of life on preferentialism between the white and the black in complexion]
94. *Nuzūl 'Īsā ibn Maryam ākhir al-zamān* (1985) [The descent of Jesus son of Maryam at the end of time]
95. *al-Qawl al-jalī fī faḍā'il 'Alī* (1990) [The manifest discourse on the virtues of 'Alī b. Abī Ṭālib ؓ]
96. *al-Radd 'alā man akhlada ilā al-arḍ wa-jahila anna al-ijtihāda fī kulli 'aṣrin farḍ* (1984) [Refutation of the shiftless who have no idea that scholarly striving is a religious obligation in every age]
97. *al-Raḥma fīl-ṭibb wal-ḥikma* (1970) [Mercy in medicine and wisdom], a spurious attribution.
98. *al-Rasā'il al-'ashr* (1989) [Ten epistles]
99. *Raṣf al-la'āl fī waṣf al-hilāl* (1890) [The stringing of the pearls in describing the new moon]
100. *al-Rawḍ al-anīq fī faḍl al-ṣiddīq* (1990) [The beautiful garden of the merit of Abū Bakr al-Ṣiddīq ؓ]
101. *Risālat al-sayf al-qāṭi' al-lāmi' li ahl al-i'tirāḍ al-shawā'i'* (1935) [Epistle of the sharp and glistening sword against the Shī'ī naysayers]
102. *al-Riyāḍ al-anīqa fī sharḥ asmā' khayr al-khalīqa* ﷺ [The beautiful gardens: explanation of the names of the best of creation ﷺ]. In the introduction to this dictionary on the names of the Prophet ﷺ, he said: "It is my hope that Allah accept this book and that through this book I shall gain the Prophet's ﷺ intercession. Perhaps it shall be that Allah make it the seal of all my works, and grant me what I have asked Him with longing regarding the Honorable One ﷺ." He also wrote *al-Bahjat al-bahiyya fil-asmā' al-nabawiyya* on the same topic.

103. *Ṣawn al-manṭiq wal-kalām ʻan fann al-manṭiq wal-kalām* (1947) [Manual of logic and dialectic theology]
104. *Sharḥ shawāhid al-mughnī* (1904) [Commentary on the proof texts of (ʻAbd Allāh b. Hishām's) *Mughnī (al-labīb*—The sufficient knowledge of the sensible one)]
105. *Sharḥ al-ṣudūr bi sharḥ ḥāl al-mawtā wal-qubūr* (1989) [The expanding of breasts, or, Commentary on the state of the dead in the graves]
106. *Sharḥ al-urjūza al-musammāt bi-ʻuqūd al-jumān fī ʻālam al-maʻānī wal-bayān* (1955) [The commentary in *rajaz* ("surging") meter entitled: The pearl necklaces related to the world of meanings and precious discourse]
107. *Shaqā'iq al-utrunj fī raqā'iq al-ghunj* (1988) [The citron halves in the daintiness of women]
108. *Shurūṭ al-mufassir wa-ādābuh* (1994) [The criteria to be met by commentators of Qur'an and their ethics]
109. *Sihām al-iṣāba fīl-daʻawāt al-mustajāba* (1987) [The arrows that hit their target: about the prayers that are fulfilled]
110. *al-Subul al-jaliyya fīl-ābā' al-ʻaliyya* (1916) [The manifest paths concerning the lofty ancestors (of the Prophet ﷺ)]
111. *Taʻaqqubāt al-Suyūṭī ʻalā mawduʻat Ibn al-Jawzī* (1886) [al-Suyūṭī's critique of Ibn al-Jawzī's collection of forged narrations]
112. *Ṭabaqāt al-mufassirīn* (1976) [The synchronical layers of Qur'an commentators]
113. *Tabyīḍ al-ṣaḥīfa bi manāqib al-Imām Abī Ḥanīfa* (1992) [The whitening of the page, or, The virtues of Imam Abū Ḥanīfa]
114. *al-Tadhyīl wal-tadhnīb ʻalā al-nihāya fī gharīb al-ḥadīth wal-āthar* (1982) [Marginal annotations on Ibn al-Athīr's "The goal"]
115. *Tadrīb al-rāwī fī sharḥ taqrīb al-Nawawī* (1994) [The training of the hadith transmitter: an exegesis of Nawawī's "The facilitation"]
116. *Tahdhīb al-khaṣā'iṣ al-nabawiyya al-kubrā* (1989) [The emendation of al-Suyūṭī's book entitled "The awesome characteristics of the Prophet ﷺ"]
117. *Taḥdhīr al-khawāṣṣ min akādhib al-quṣṣāṣ* (1932) [Warning the elite against the lies of storytellers]. In this work al-Suyūṭī recapitulates and builds on the work of al-ʻIrāqī (725–806), *al-Bāʻith ʻalā*

al-khalāṣ min ḥawādith al-quṣṣāṣ, which excoriates the misuse of hadith by semi-educated shaykhs and imams and critiques the same-themed *al-Quṣṣāṣ wal-mudhakkirīn* by Ibn al-Jawzī and *Aḥādīth al-quṣṣāṣ* by Aḥmad b. Taymiyya.

118. *Takhrīj aḥādīth sharḥ al-mawāqif fī 'ilm al-kalām* (1986) [The documentation of the hadith mentioned in "The commentary of the stopping-places in dialectical theology," a work by al-Qāḍī 'Aḍuḍ al-Dīn 'Abd al-Raḥmān b. Aḥmad al-Ījī al-Shīrāzī (d. 756)].
119. *Tamhīd al-farsh fīl-khiṣāl al-mūjiba li-ẓilāl al-'arsh* (1990) [The characteristics that guarantee the shading of the throne]
120. *Tanbīh al-ghabī fī takhṭi'at Ibn 'Arabī* (1990) [Warning to the imbecile who imputes error to Muḥyī al-Dīn ibn 'Arabī (a reply to al-Biqā'ī's "Warning to the Imbecile that Ibn 'Arabī is a disbeliever")]
121. *Tanwīr al-ḥawālik sharḥ 'alā Muwaṭṭa' Mālik* (1969) [The enlightenment of intense blackness: commentary on Mālik's *Muwaṭṭa'*]; with *Is'āf al-mubaṭṭa' fī rijāl al-Muwaṭṭa'* [Rescuing those stalled concerning the narrators of Mālik's *Muwaṭṭa'*]
122. *Tanwīr al-miqbās min tafsīr Ibn 'Abbās* (1951) [The enlightenment of torchlights from the Qur'anic commentary of Ibn 'Abbās]
123. *Tanzīh al-anbiyā' 'an tashbīh al-aghbiyā'* (1916) [Clearing the prophets from the comparisons ignorant people make of themselves with them]
124. *Taqrīr al-istinād fī tafsīr al-ijtihād* (1983) [Establishing authoritative ascription in the course of scholarly striving]
125. *al-Ta'rīf bi-ādāb al-ta'līf* (1989) [The etiquette of authorship]
126. *Tārīkh al-khulafā'* (1993) [History of the caliphs]
127. *Tartīb suwar al-Qur'ān* (1986) [The ordering of the suras of the Qur'an]
128. *Tasliyat al-ābā' bi-fuqdān al-abnā' al-musammāt al-ta'allul wal-iṭfā' li-nārin la yuṭfa'* (1987) [The consolation of parents who have lost their children, also known as, The extinction of the unquenchable fire]
129. *Ṭawq al-ḥamāma* (1988) [The flight of the dove]
130. *Ta'yīd al-ḥaqīqat al-'aliyya wa-tashyīd al-ṭarīqa al-Shādhiliyya* (1934) [The upholding of the lofty truth and the buttressing of the Shādhilī sufi path]

131. *al-Taʿẓīm wal-minna fī anna abaway rasūlallāh fīl-janna* (1916) [That the Prophet's parents are in paradise]
132. *Tazyīn al-mamālik bi-manāqib sayyidinā Mālik* (1907) [The adornment of slaves with the virtues of Imam Mālik]
133. *Tuḥfat al-abrār bi-nukat al-adhkār līl-Nawawī* (1990) [Commentary on Nawawī's "Supplications"]
134. *Tuḥfat al-ʿajlān fī faḍā'il ʿUthmān* (1991) [Merits of ʿUthmān b. ʿAffān]
135. *Tuḥfat al-nujabā'* (1990) [The gem of patricians (a work on language)]
136. *ʿUqūd al-zabarjad ʿalā musnad al-Imām Aḥmad* (1987) [The chrysolite necklaces on Imam Aḥmad's collection of narrations (traced to the Prophet ﷺ)]
137. *ʿUqūd al-zabarjad fī iʿrāb al-ḥadīth al-nabawī* (1994) [The chrysolite necklaces on the grammatical analysis of the Prophet's narrations], on the *Musnad* of Aḥmad b. Ḥanbal. This is the same work as in the previous entry.
138. *al-Wasā'il fī musāmarat al-awā'il* (1986) [The means for conversation with the ancients]; also published as *al-Wasā'il ilā maʿrifat al-awa'il* (1990) [The means to the acquaintance of the ancients]
139. *Wuṣūl al-amānī bi uṣūl al-tahānī* (1987) [The attainment of one's hope in the etiquette of well-wishing]
140. *al-Zajru bil-hijr* (1950) [The reprimand by means of the reminder of what is unlawful]
141. *Zubdat al-laban fawā'id lughawiyya wa-ḥadīthiyya* (1989) [The cream of the milk: benefits related to language and hadith]

APPENDIX II

ḤANAFĪ FATWAS ON LOUD *DHIKR* IN THE MOSQUE

According to Imams Khayr al-Dīn al-Ramlī in his *Fatāwā khayriyya*, al-Ḥaskafī in the *Durr al-mukhtār*, al-Nābulusī in *Jami' al-asrār*, al-Lacknawī in *Sibāḥat al-fikr*, Ibn 'Ābidīn in his *Ḥāshiyya*, and Aḥmad Rashīd Gangohī in his *Fatāwā rashīdiyya*, the correct position of the Ḥanafi school is that loud *dhikr* is permissible. In this respect the Ḥanafī position is in line with the other three schools.

Khayr al-Dīn al-Ramlī's Discussion

Imam Khayr al-Dīn al-Ramlī said:

> [Concerning] what the Sufi masters took as a custom in holding circles of *dhikr* and making loud congregational *dhikr* in the mosques from generation to generation, reciting poems authored by the possessors of Divine wisdoms such as the Qādiriyya and Sa'diyya and Muṭawwi'a among those acknowledged and accepted by the *fuqahā'* of the Muslim community, and they say: O Shaykh 'Abd al-Qādir! O Shaykh Aḥmad [al-Badawī]! O Rifā'ī! Something for the sake of God (*shay'un lillāh*) O 'Abd al-Qādir! and such, at which time they become greatly entranced and experience states that make them jump up and down, etc.
>
> He answered—God have mercy on him: "Know first of all that among the famous rules that are firmly put to use in the books of the imams is the rule that matters are judged according to their ends [. . .]

> as taken from the hadith of the Two Shaykhs al-Bukhārī and Muslim: 'Actions are only according to intentions'[. . .] and none denies the reality of the Sufis except every ignorant, foolish soul. As for the circles of *dhikr* and making loud *dhikr* and reciting poems, there is evidence in the hadith that entails loud *dhikr* such as the narration: 'And if he mentions me in a gathering, I mention him in a better gathering'[1] [. . .] And the mention of Him in a gathering is not in any other way than out loud, and the same goes for the circles of *dhikr* and their circumambulation by the angels."[2]

Imam Ibn Ḥajar al-Haytamī al-Makkī al-Shāfiʿī gave a similar reply to a question on the *dhikr* practices of Sufis after congregational prayers in the mosques and the recitation of poetry by the Sufi masters.[3]

Ibn ʿĀbidīn's First Discussion

Imam Ibn ʿĀbidīn said in his *Ḥāshiyya:* "The text of the *Bazzāziyya* [regarding loud *dhikr*] has inconsistencies.[4] First, it quotes from the *Fatāwā* of the Qadi [Khān] that 'it [loud dhikr] is *ḥarām* due to the sound[5] report from Ibn Masʿūd that he expelled a group from the mosque that were saying *lā ilāha illā Allāh* and invoking *ṣalawāt* out loud and that he said to them, "I do not think you are anything but innovators." ' " Then al-Bazzāzī said:

> And also considering what was narrated in the *Ṣaḥīḥ* that he ﷺ said to those that were raising their voices saying *Allāhu akbar*: "Be gentle on yourselves for you are not calling upon one who is deaf or absent but you are calling upon one who is hearing and seeing and near just as He is with you."[6] It is possible that there was no advantage then to raising voices for it was narrated that they were in the midst of a military campaign, and perhaps raising their voices would have caused them harm, because war is ruse.[7] This is why ringing bells was forbidden in military campaigns. As for raising the voice in *dhikr*, it is allowed (*jā'iz*) just as in *adhān*, *khuṭba*, *jumuʿa*, etc.

"He [al-Ramlī] probed the issue in depth in the [*Fatāwā*] *khayriyya* and interpreted what is found in the qadi's *Fatāwā* to mean the harmful kind of loudness, saying: "There are hadiths that demand loudness and hadiths that demand secrecy...the latter is preferable when self-display (*riyā'*) is feared or if it harms those who are praying or sleeping, while loudness is otherwise preferable."[8]

al-Ḥaskafī's Permissions

The great Damascene Ḥanafī Imam 'Alā' al-Dīn Muḥammad b. 'Alī b. Muḥammad b. 'Alī b. 'Abd al-Raḥmān b. Muḥammad al-Ḥiṣnī al-Ḥaskafī[9] (1025–1088 AH) in his major work *al-Durr al-mukhtār*, his commentary on al-Ghazzī al-Tumurtāshī's (d. 1004 AH) *Tanwīr al-abṣār wa-jāmi' al-biḥār*, states:

> To beg in the mosque is *ḥarām* while giving is *makrūh*, in absolute terms, and it was also said: [only] if one steps over people's shoulders. So is to announce that something has been lost or recite poetry except what contains *dhikr*, or raising the voice with *dhikr* except for students of *fiqh* [...][10]

Note: his earlier namesake the Shāfi'ī *faqīh* and philologist Shams al-Dīn Abū al-Luṭf Muḥammad b. 'Alī b. Manṣūr b. Zayn al-'Arab al-Ḥaskafī al-Ḥiṣnī (819–859 AH) authored an eight-page fatwa on *dhikr* in which he defends not only the practice of loud *dhikr* in mosques but the practice of the Sufi *ḥaḍra*. The fatwa begins with the following question and reply:

> Q. "What is the position of the imams of the religion [...] regarding what the *mutaṣawwifa* do of *dhikr* in a standing position and loudness in *dhikr* [...]?
>
> A. As for the standing *dhikr*, its merit is unquestionable, but *dhikr* sitting is better because of what some of the accomplished verifiers have said [...]"[11]

Ibn 'Ābidīn's Second Discussion

Ibn 'Ābidīn comments on the above passage of the *Durr*:

"Concerning his statement: 'or raising the voice with *dhikr,* etc.' I say, there is inconsistency in the words of the author of the [*Fatāwā*] *bazzāziyya* in this. One time he states that it is categorically prohibited (*ḥarām*) and another time he states that it is permissible (*jā'iz*). Whereas in the discussion of the *Fatāwā khayriyya* whether it is disliked or approved it says:

> There is evidence in the hadith that entails the requirement of loud *dhikr* such as [the narration]: "And if he mentions me in a gathering, I mention him in a better gathering."[12] The two shaykhs narrated iṭ And there is other evidence that entails the requirement of soft *dhikr*. The agreement between them is that this differs according to situation and persons just as in the case of the narrations of loudness and softness in recitation (*qirā'a*). Nor is this [agreement] contradicted by the hadith, "The best *dhikr* is the silent one,"[13] as the latter applies when self-display is feared, or causing nuisance to those who are praying or sleeping. If those aspects are avoided, then some of the people of knowledge said that loud *dhikr* is better because it comprises more *'amal* and because its benefit is extended to those that hear it, and the heart of the person making *dhikr* is awakened so that his outward act is paired with his reflection, his listening is monopolized by *dhikr*, drowsiness is eliminated, and energy increased.

"This is the gist of what he said and the complete text is there, so be sure to read it."

"It was also mentioned in *Ḥāshiyat al-ḥamawī*, quoting Imam al-Sha'rānī: 'The ulama of the *salaf* and *khalaf* concur on the desirability of congregational *dhikr* in the mosques and elsewhere unless their loudness cause nuisance on those that are sleeping, praying, or reading, etc.'"

al-Ḥalabī's Attack on the Sufis

Imam Ibrāhīm al-Ḥalabī authored *al-Rahṣ wal-waqṣ li-mustaḥill al-raqṣ* against the practice of the *ḥaḍra*, a slim book recently republished by two rabid Damascene anti-Sufis, Ḥasan al-Samāḥī Suwaydān and the late 'Abd al-Qādir al-Arna'ūṭ in which the claim of Qadi Khān's *Fatāwā* is reiterated.[14]

al-Shurunbulālī's Rejection of al-Ḥalabī's Fatwa

Imam al-Shurunbulālī said, as quoted in al-Nābulusī's *Jam' al-asrār*:

> What was said in an epistle attributed to 'Allāma al-Ḥalabī and others prohibiting it [standing and moving during *dhikr,* e.g. Shādhilīs] and declaring *kāfir* whoever permits it, or adds the drum and wind instrument to it: this fatwa is incorrect [. . .] as for raising the voice in *dhikr,* there is a difference of opinion over it among our [Ḥanafī] imams, Qadi Khān in his *Fatāwā* mentioned its offensive character while [Ibn Manṣūr] the author of *al-Baḥr* cited from *al-Qinya* [*Qinyat al-fatāwā* by al-Zāhidī], after citing Qadi Khān, that "there is no harm in it but it is better to keep it soft."[15]

al-Nābulusī's Summation

Shaykh 'Abd al-Ghanī al-Nābulusī's long and comprehensive fatwa titled *Jam' al-asrār fī radd al-ṭa'ni 'an al-ṣūfiyyat al-akhyār ahl al-tawājud bil-adhkār* [The compendium of secrets: refutation of the criticism made against the elect Sufis, the people of emotional swaying with *dhikr*] which also recently received an edition by the Damascene Hibat al-Māliḥ that cites practically all the positions for and against in the four schools and their proofs. He concludes that the correct position is that loud congregational *dhikr* in the mosque is absolutely permissible.

al-Qārī's Agreement with the Sufis

Al-Qārī in his Sufi treatise *Fatḥ abwāb al-dīn fī ādāb al-murīdīn* agrees with al-Shurunbulālī and al-Nābulusī as per his chapter on *samā'* which begins, "As for dancing (*raqṣ*), even though it is a kind of defect (*naqṣ*), some said it is disliked while others said it is permissible, among them al-Rāfi'ī, al-Ghazzālī, al-Nawawī [. . .]."[16]

al-Lacknawī's Fatwa

In his similar fatwa in support of loud *dhikr* titled *Sibāḥat al-fikr fīl-jahri bil-dhikr*, published by Shaykh 'Abd al-Fattāḥ Abū Ghudda, Imam

'Abd al-Ḥayy al-Lacknawī examines the inconsistency of the Ḥanafī positions over the issue and confirms that the *Fatāwā khayriyya* forwards the most correct one:

> These are the positions of our colleagues, so consider them and see how inconsistent and divergent their opinions are, one saying it is permissible, the other *ḥarām*,[17] the other *bid'a*, and the other *makrūh*, the most correct position being permissibility (*jawāz*) as long as it does not trespass limits, as chosen by al-Khayr al-Ramlī.[18]

Gangohī's Fatwa

In his *Fatāwā rashīdiyya* he replies to the question, "Is loud *dhikr* permissible or impermissible in the Ḥanafī School?" saying, "There is a difference of opinion in the matter regarding loud *dhikr* in the books of Ḥanafī *fiqh*, some regarding it as disliked on such occasions where it is not warranted, while others regard it as permissible, and this is the preferred position."[19]

Ibn 'Ābidīn's Third Endorsement of Loud Group Dhikr

Ibn 'Ābidīn also said of loud group *dhikr*: "Imam al-Ghazzālī compared doing *dhikr* alone and the *dhikr* of a group to the *adhān* of someone alone and the *adhān* of a group. He said, 'As the voices of a group of muezzins reach farther than the voice of a single muezzin, so the *dhikr* of a group on one heart has more effect in lifting dense veils than the *dhikr* of a single person.'"[20]

al-Ṭaḥṭāwī's Endorsement of Loud Group Dhikr

Al-Ṭaḥṭāwī said in his commentary on al-Shurunbulālī's *Marāqī al-falāḥ:*

> The author of the *Fatāwā* said: "None can be forbidden from making *dhikr* out loud in the mosques lest the one forbidding it come under the saying of God Most High, *And who does greater wrong than he who forbids the approach to the sanctuaries of God lest His name should be mentioned therein* [. . .]? (Qur'an 2:114)." Thus in the *Bazzāziyya*.

Al-Sha'rānī stipulated in *Dhikr al-dhākir lil-madhkūr wal-shākir lil-mashkūr* verbatim: "The ulama of the *salaf* and *khalf* unanimously agree on the desirability of remembering God Most High in a group in the mosques and elsewhere without any objection unless their *dhikr* aloud disturbs someone sleeping, praying, or reciting the Qur'an, as is confirmed in the books of *fiqh*."[21]

Understanding the Hadiths against Raising of the Voice in the Mosque

Some hadiths are misconstrued as proofs for prohibiting loud *dhikr* in the mosque:

1. Our liege-lord, al-Sā'ib b. Yazīd ﷺ said that someone threw a pebble at him as he stood in the mosque, whereupon he turned and saw it was our liege-lord 'Umar ﷺ. The latter told him to call a certain two persons to him. When the two were brought he asked: "Where are you from?" "Ṭā'if," they replied. 'Umar said: "Had you been from this country [Madīna], I would have certainly made the two of you sore! How dare you raise your voices in the mosque of the Messenger of God ﷺ?"[22]

   The meaning of voices in this report is that of *laghṭ*—clatter and meaningless noise or babble as elucidated from the narration of 'Abd al-Razzāq adduced by Ibn Ḥajar in the explanation of the above report: "'Umar used to forbid them to make noise (*al-laghṭ*) in the mosque."[23] Compare this state of dignity and quiet in the august presence of the Prophet ρ to the present time, when the noise of vendors and their radios reach inside the Ḥaram al-Sharīf in Madīna without obstacle, while those who greet and recite *ṣalawāt* on the Prophet ﷺ are thrown out and humiliated!
2. The hadith of the fifteen signs preceding the day of resurrection, among which the Prophet said ﷺ as reported by our liege-lords 'Alī and Abū Hurayra ﷺ "voices shall be raised in the mosques."[24]

This means "in disputes, transactions, idle pastimes, and play" as per al-Mubārakfūrī in his commentary on al-Tirmidhī titled *Tuḥfat al-aḥwadhī,* to which can be added the proclamation of lost items as illustrated by Ibn Ḥibbān's narration of the hadith to that effect in his *Ṣaḥīḥ* under the subheading "The rebuke against raising voices in the mosques for matters of this evanescent world."[25]

3. The same worldly meanings are meant in the report that banishes loud voices from the mosque with the wording "Keep away from your mosques your young boys, madmen, buying and selling, quarrels, loud voices [. . .]" although this report is inauthentic.[26]

And God Most High knows best.

APPENDIX III

DHIKR "ALLAH, ALLAH"

The question is sometimes asked whether it is permissible to make *dhikr* by repeating the name of God alone, saying "Allah, Allah, Allah [. . .]" without any accompanying phrase or construct such as *subḥān Allāh, al-ḥamdu lillah, Allāhu akbar, lā ilāha illā Allāh* or with a vocative form ("*Yā Allāh*"), etc.

The proofs of this begin with the glorious Qur'an: *Say: Allah Then leave them to their playing* (Qur'an 6:91); *Surely by mentioning Allah hearts become peaceful* (Qur'an 13:28).

Then come all the hadiths in al-Suyūṭī's fatwa mentioning that one makes mention (*dhikr*) of Allah, i.e., the literal mention of His name, as the foremost principle in the Arabic language is that words are primarily understood literally unless there is an impediment to doing so.

In addition, our liege-lord, 'Abd Allāh b. Mughaffal ﵁ mentioned that the Messenger of God ﷺ said:

> Allah, Allah! Fear Him regarding my companions! Do not make them targets after me! Whoever loves them loves them with his love for me; and whoever hates them hates them with his hatred for me. Whoever bears enmity for them, bears enmity for me; and whoever bears enmity for me, bears enmity for God. And whoever bears enmity for God is about to perish![1]

Asmā' bint 'Umays, the wife of our liege-lord Abū Bakr and mother of 'Abd Allāh b. Ja'far b. Abī Ṭālib—﵃—said: "The Messenger of God ﷺ taught me words for me to say in times of duress: 'Allah, Allah is my Lord nor do I associate with him anything!'"[2] 'Ā'isha, Thawbān, and others narrate the same as a special instruction to the Prophet's family ﷺ.[3] Imam al-Nawawī's daily devotion (*wird*) uses this very *dhikr* as narrated to us by the late Shaykh Muḥammad b. 'Alawī al-Mālikī and others ﷺ.

Anas ﷺ mentioned that the Messenger of God ﷺ said: "The hour will not rise until Allah, Allah! is no longer said on the earth."

Another version of the same states: "The hour will not rise on anyone saying: Allah, Allah."[4]

Muslim narrated both in his *Ṣaḥīḥ,* "Book of *īmān,*" chapter 66 titled (by al-Nawawī): "The disappearance of belief at the end of times."

Imam al-Nawawī said in his commentary on this chapter: "Know that the narrations of this hadith are unanimous in the repetition of the name of God the Exalted for both versions and that is the way it is found in all the authoritative books."[5]

Note that Imam al-Nawawī placed Anas' hadith under the heading of the disappearance of belief (*īmān*) at the end of time although there is no mention of belief in the hadith. This shows that saying "Allah, Allah" stands for belief. Those who say it have belief, while those who do not say it do not have belief. Those who fight those who say it are actually worse than those who merely lack belief and do not say "Allah, Allah!"

Note also that al-Nawawī highlights the authenticity of the repetition of the form to establish that the words "Allah, Allah" are a *sunna ma'thūra* or invocation inherited from the Prophet ﷺ and his companions as it stands. This makes it clear that Shaykh Aḥmad ibn Taymiyya's claim—in purported refutation of Imam al-Ghazzālī—that the words must not be used alone but obligatorily in construct on pain of innovation[6] is itself unsubstantiated. Further, one who knows that the *dhikr* "Allah, Allah" has been mentioned by the Messenger of God ﷺ is not at liberty to dispute it on the grounds that the companions did not use it. It suffices for its licit basis that the Prophet said it ﷺ.

Nor can one object to similar forms of single-name *dhikr* such as *Huwa*, *Ḥayy* and *Ḥaqq*. *To God belong the most beautiful names, so call Him by them* (Qur'an 7:180). It is established that our liege-lord

Bilal used to make the single-name, repetitive dhikr "*Aḥad, Aḥad*" while being dragged by boys through the mountains of Makka with a rope around his neck.[7] As for the hadith of the ninety-nine names, it does not limit the names of God to only ninety-nine, as al-Nawawī, al-Qurṭubī, Ibn Nāṣir al-Dīn, and others made clear in their commentaries of that hadith.

Note that the Siddiqi translation of *Ṣaḥīḥ Muslim*, which is almost as flawed as the Khan translation of *Ṣaḥīḥ al-Bukhari* mistranslates the first as: "The hour (resurrection) would not come so long as God is supplicated in the world" and the second as "The hour (resurrection) would not come upon anyone so long as he supplicates God." This is wrong as translation goes, although it is right as a commentary, since saying "Allah, Allah" is supplicating Him, as is all worship according to the hadith of the Prophet: "Supplication is worship itself."[8] However, with regard to accuracy in translation, the word form highlighted by al-Nawawī must be kept intact in any explanation of this hadith. It is not generically "supplicating God" but specifically saying: "Allah, Allah" according to the Prophet's own wording, . Nor does the fact that an alternate version exists outside the *Ṣaḥīḥ* with the words *la ilaha illā Allāh* instead of "Allah, Allah" in any way cancel out the wording in Muslim.

Sahl al-Tustarī said: "There are three types of eaters: one eats light and faith from the start of his food to the end; one eats nothing but food; and one eats dung (*sirjīn*). The first one names Allah at the beginning, remembers Him with every bite, and thanks Him at the end; the second one names Him at the beginning and thanks Him at the end; the third one neither names Him nor thanks Him nor remembers Him."

Shāh Bahā' al-Dīn Naqshband reportedly said: "This path is built upon breath," meaning God-consciousness, death to the world, presence of heart, and the remembrance of Allah with every breath. God sanctify his secret and benefit us with him. A Muslim scientist wrote, "During the average human lifespan, a person will breathe five hundred million times."[9]

Imam al-Ghazzālī said in his masterpiece, *Iḥyā' 'ulūm al-dīn* (3:19–20), in the section on destructive sins (*muhlikāt*), "Book of the wonders of the heart," chapter on "The difference between inspiration and learning," describing *dhikr*, as cited by al-Khānī in his great summation *al-Bahjat al-saniyya fi ādāb al-ṭarīqat al-Naqshbandiyya:*

> He secludes himself, doing no more than the obligatory worships (*farā'iḍ*) and their non-obligatory additions (*rawātib*). He does not distract his thoughts (while performing the following *dhikr*) by reciting the Qur'an nor reflecting about *tafsīr*, books of hadith, or other subjects. On the contrary, he makes an effort that none but God Most High crosses his mind.
>
> After sitting in seclusion, he persists in continuously saying with the tongue "Allah, Allah" with presence of heart until he ends up in a state where he quits moving the tongue and sees as if the word is still running over his tongue. He perseveres until its traces disappear from the tongue yet he finds his heart continuing the *dhikr*.[10]
>
> Then he perseveres with this until the image of the expression [Allah], its letters, and the form of the word are erased from the heart, while the meaning of the word remains alone in his heart, present therein, as if established in the heart and not leaving it.
>
> He has the choice to reach this limit and the choice to preserve this state by repelling away *waswasa* but he has no choice after that in acquiring the subsequent mercy of God: he became, as a result of what he did, exposed to the bestowing breezes of the mercy of God! So what remains is but to wait for what mercy God may open up, as He opened it up upon the prophets and *awliyā'* in this manner.
>
> Then, if his resolve (*irāda*) is truthful and his determination pure, and if he perseveres well, such that his desires do not keep pulling him and his internal prattle about worldly bonds does not distract him,[11] then the lights of truth shall shine in his heart!
>
> This will initially be unstable like swift lightning. Then it will return and may linger. If this returns, it may persist and it may also be short. If it persists, it may be for a long while, and it may be for a short duration. Similar but different states may follow each other, or it may only be one type, and the levels therein of the friends of God are countless just as their individual natures and moral features are countless.
>
> This method goes back to nothing more than purification, cleansing and polishing on your part, followed only by readiness and waiting.[12]

Our master, the light of our eyes, the treasure of this world, Mawlānā al-Shaykh Nāẓim said in the talks transcribed from him under the title *From Dunyā to Mawlā*:

> The first condition for protection is to believe in God and the second to continue worshipping. Run and put down your prayer-carpet, pray, make *dhikr*, and glorify the Lord. There is no protection left now except that. Even whole armies cannot protect one single person [. . .]
>
> God likes and orders to be glorified. It gives power and peace to you. Try to say more: *Lā ilāha illā Allāh*, say: Allah, Allah, make *ṣalawāt* on the Prophet ﷺ.
>
> Try to give more time of your day to reach to spiritual power. Every worshipping and *dhikr* helps, giving you more love for the Lord, and real life comes through love. Saints say: people without love are like dead ones walking on earth.
>
> Love is life, light and our perfection. As much as your love is growing, you live more enjoyful and happier. *The main purpose of ṭarīqas is to train people to make dhikr, so that they may take support and power from it.*
>
> The time of *qiyāma* is approaching now. Hundreds of signs have appeared and one of them is that people leave glorification of the Lord. And sufferings rain down on them. Then they ask treatment by drugs.
>
> All illnesses go away by glorifying the Lord. Through your love for the Lord you will reach health, pleasure and happiness here and hereafter."
>
> And God knows best.

Blessings and peace on our liege-lord the
Prophet Muḥammad ﷺ his family,
and all his companions. All
praise belongs to God
the Lord of the
worlds

NOTES

Publisher's Note

1. Take for example, Imam al-Ṭabarī's (d. 310/971) *Tafsīr* spanning some ten thousand pages and consisting of 30 volumes; the massive 80 volume biographical dictionary, *Tarīkh madīnat Dimashq* of 'Alī b. al-Ḥasan b. 'Asakir (d. 571/1175); Imam al-Qurṭubī's (d. 671/1273) *al-Jāmi' li aḥkām al-Qur'ān* consisting of 20 volumes and the *Siyar a'lām al-nubalā'* written by Muḥammad Shams al-Dīn al-Dhahabī (d. 748/1348) consisting of 23 volumes. Not only did Muslim scholars write multi-volume works, but also the overall quantity of books that the medieval scholars produced was staggering.
2. *Dhikr* has many meanings, which include the Qur'an and its recitation, prayer, learning, and teaching, etc. While some Muslims simply restrict *dhikr* to aspects just noted, this book examines the last two categories of the meaning of *dhikr*, namely the "invocation of God with the tongue according to one of the formulas taught by the Messenger of God ﷺ or any other formula, and the remembrance of God in the heart, or in both the heart and the tongue."
3. Related by Muslim in his *Ṣaḥīḥ*.
4. The hadith reads: Abū Sa'īd narrates that the Messenger of God ﷺ was asked, "Which of the servants of God is best in rank before Him on the day of resurrection?" He replied: "The ones who remember him much." I said: "O Messenger of God, what about the fighter in the way of God?" He answered: "Even if he strikes the disbelievers and polytheists with his sword until it broke, and becomes red with their blood, truly those who do the remembrance of God are better than him in rank." Related by Aḥmad, Tirmidhī, and Bayhaqī. For a detailed discussion on verses from the Qur'an and various hadiths that deal with fighting, see David Dakake,

"The Myth of a Militant Islam," in Aftab Ahmad Malik (ed.,) *The State We are In: Identity, Terror and the Law of Jihad* (Bristol: Amal Press, 2008). This essay draws extensively upon early traditional Qur'anic exegesis while also providing an historical analysis of the "actual forms of the earliest jihad and the conduct of the *mujāhidūn*, the fighters in jihad, as exemplified by the Prophet of Islam and his successors." To see how warfare is regulated and limits established from the Qur'an and the hadith, see Suheil Laher, "Indiscriminate Killing in Light of Islamic Sacred Texts" (Ibid.).

5. 'Abd Allāh b. 'Umar narrates that the Messenger of God ﷺ used to say: "Everything has a polish, and the polish of heart is the remembrance of God. Nothing is more valuable to rescue from God's punishment than the remembrance of God." He was asked whether this did not apply also to jihad in God's path, and he replied: "Not even if one should ply his sword until it breaks." Related by Bayhaqī, in *Mishkat al-masabih.*
6. al-Bukhāri, *Kitāb al-riqāq*, (11:308) and Muslim, *Kitāb al-imān,* (2:18). The complete hadith is: "Let whoever believes in God and the Last Day either speak good or remain silent; and let whoever believes in God and the last day be generous to his neighbor; and let whoever believes in God and the Last Day be generous to his guest."
7. The hadith states that: "A man came to the Prophet and said, 'O Messenger of God! The laws and conditions of Islam have become too many for me. Tell me something that I can always keep.' The Prophet ﷺ said: 'Keep your tongue moist with the remembrance of God.' " Narrated by Aḥmad, Tirmidhī, and Ibn Mājah. Ibn Ḥibban declared it fair (*hasan*).

Biography of Imam al-Suyūṭī

1. See Appendix I for a partial list of his published works.
2. Cf. al-Suyūṭī's vitriolic tract *al-Kāwī fil-radd 'alā al-Sakhāwī* [The searing brand in refuting al-Sakhāwī] and his unflattering mention in the poem *Naẓm al-'iqyān fī a'yān al-a'yān*. Al-Sakhāwī also wrote unflatteringly of al-Suyūṭī in his *Ḍaw' al-lāmi*. They were both prolific Shāfi'ī, Shādhilī, Ash'arī hadith masters and students of *Amīr al-mu'minīn fil-ḥadīth* Ibn Ḥajar al-'Asqalānī. The ulama prohibit looking into the disputes between contemporaries and command the Muslims to ignore them. Only those who seek *fitna* probe them.

3. Muḥammad b. Ibrāhīm al-Shaybānī and Aḥmad al-Khazindar, eds. *Dalīl makhṭūṭāt al-Suyūṭī*, 2nd ed. (Kuwait: Manshurat Markaz al-Makhtutat, 1995).
4. al-ʿAjlūnī in *Kashf al-khafā'* states that this hadith is narrated by al-Ṭabarānī in *al-Awsaṭ* from Ibn ʿUmar rather than the Prophet ﷺ, and that al-Haytamī said in his *Fatāwā ḥadīthiyya* that it is actually a saying of (the *tābiʿī*) Yaḥyā b. Kathīr.
5. In al-Kattānī, *Fahras al-fahāris wal-athbāt* (2:1012).
6. al-Suyūṭī, *Ṭabaqāt al-ḥuffāẓ* (p. 518).
7. al-Suyūṭī, *Ḥusn al-muḥāḍara fī akhbār Miṣr wal-Qāhira* (p. 157).
8. al-Suyūṭī, *al-Radd ʿalā man akhlada ilā al-ard* (p. 116).
9. Ibn Ḥajar, *al-Muʿjam* (p. 400 §1774).
10. See the entry of the *Tadhkira* in the bibliography.
11. The pious Sevillian imam and hadith master, Abū al-Qāsim Abū Zayd ʿAbd al-Raḥmān b. ʿAbd Allāh b. Aḥmad al-Suhaylī (508–581 AH). He became blind at seventeen and went on to become an authority in history, the canonical readings, and Arabic. He authored *al-Rawḍ al-unuf fī sharḥ gharīb al-siyar*, a vast commentary on Ibn Isḥāq's *Sīra*, in which he said he summed up about 120 books. Al-Dhahabī documents him in his *Tārikh* (*ann.* 581–590: 113–116 §21) and *Tadhkirat al-ḥuffāẓ* (4:1348–1350 §1099).
12. Translation courtesy of Musa Furber.
13. See, for example, al-Sakhāwī's words in his *Maqāṣid*, in the entry *khirqa*.
14. Ibn Abī Yaʿlā, *Ṭabaqāt al-ḥanābila* (1:192): "My father (al-Qāḍī Abū Yaʿlā) narrated to me in writing: ʿĪsā b. Muḥammad b. ʿAlī narrated to us: I heard ʿAbd Allāh b. Muḥammad (Imam Abū al-Qāsim al-Baghawī) say: I heard Abū ʿAbd Allāh Aḥmad b. Muḥammad b. Ḥanbal say: 'al-Ḥasan did narrate (*qad rawa*) from ʿAlī b. Abī Ṭālib.'" For the listing of the chains of transmission establishing that al-Ḥasan narrated from ʿAlī see al-Suyūṭī's *Ta'yīd al-ḥaqīqa al-ʿaliyya wa-tashyīd al-ṭarīqa al-shādhiliyya* and Shaykh Aḥmad al-Ghumārī's extensive discussion in his *al-Burhān al-jalī*.
15. al-Suyūṭī, *al-Ḥāwī lil-fatāwā*. Cf. section on *dhikr* beads in al-Shawkānī's *Nayl al-awṭār* (2:316–317) and Zakariyyā al-Kandihlawī's *Ḥayāt al-ṣaḥāba*. Albānī's astounding claim that whoever carries *dhikr* beads in his hand to remember God is misguided and innovating was refuted in Maḥmūd Saʿīd's *Wuṣūl al-tahānī bi ithbāt sunniyyat al-sibḥa wal-radd ʿalā al-Albānī* [The alighting of mutual benefit and the confirmation that *dhikr* beads are a sunna in refutation of Albānī]. Another refutation was published by

Ḥāmid Mirzā Khān al-Firghānī al-Namnakānī in the seventh *mas'ala* of his *al-Masā'il al-tis'* (Madīna: Maktabat al-Īmān, 1985) p. 44–48.

16. al-Biqā'ī is Ibrāhīm b. 'Umar b. al-Ḥasan al-Dimashqī (d. 885 AH). Born and raised in the Beka valley, he moved to Damascus, then al-Quds, then Cairo, studying under the authorities of his time. Among his students were al-Haytamī who criticized him heavily for his attack on Sufis, particularly Ibn 'Arabī. Al-Sakhāwī also bore him great aversion and wrote in *al-Ḍaw' al-lāmi'* (1:101): "I do not find that he became accomplished in any of the disciplines and his works bear witness to what I said." Al-Shawkānī takes an opposite stance in *al-Badr al-ṭāli'* (p. 40–43), naming him "the great imam ... [who] shone in all the disciplines and surpassed his contemporaries"! Al-Biqā'ī was taken to task for his frequent use of the Torah and the Gospel in his *Tafsīr*. When the Mālikī qadi of Cairo almost convicted him of *kufr* he left Cairo and came to Damascus where he continued to face trials until his deat.
17. al-Biqā'ī, *Maṣra' al-taṣawwuf, aw, Tanbīh al-ghabī ilā takfīr Ibn 'Arabī,* ed. 'Abd al-Raḥmān al-Wakīl (Bilbis: Dār al-Taqwā, 1989); al-Suyūṭī, *Tanbīh al-ghabī fī takhṭi'at Ibn 'Arabī,* ed. 'Abd al-Raḥmān Ḥasan Mahmūd (Cairo: Maktabat al-Adab, 1990).
18. Al-Haytamī voices a similar fatwa in his *Fatāwā ḥadīthiyya* (p. 295–296).
19. Ibn Ḥajar said in *Inbā' al-ghumr*: "When the sayings of Ibn 'Arabī became famous in Yemen and Shaykh Ismā'īl al-Jabartī began to invite people to them and they won over the ulama of those regions, Shaykh Majd al-Dīn began to incorporate in his commentary of al-Bukhārī the words of Ibn 'Arabī in the *Futūḥāt*, which was the reason his book was concealed."
20. Cf. *Kashf al-ẓunūn* (2:1827).
21. Cf. Ibn 'Arabī, *'Aqīdat ahl al-Islām*: [167] "He perfected the making of the universe and made it uniquely excellent (*akmala ṣan'a al-'ālami wa-abda'ahu*) when He brought it into existence and invented it."
22. Cf. *Kashf al-ẓunūn* (1:408), *'Uqūd al-jawhar, Ḥusn al-muḥāḍara* (1:344), and *Hadiyyat al-'ārifīn* (1:537). Our teacher Mawlānā al-Shaykh Nāẓim said concerning al-Ghazzālī's statement that it represents the apex of good conduct with the Creator.
23. al-Haytamī, *Fatāwā ḥadīthiyya* (p. 54). An exhaustive discussion and documentation of all the scholarly positions taken on al-Ghazzālī's famous statement is given by Shaykh Aḥmad b. al-Mubārak (d. 1155 AH) in his masterpiece biography of the Ghawth Sidi 'Abd al-'Azīz al-Dabbagh

titled *al-Ibrīz min kalām sayyidi al-ghawth 'Abd al-'Azīz* (2:213–254). I did not see the work of Eric Ormsby, *Theodicy in Islamic Thought: The Dispute over al-Ghazālī's "Best of All Possible Worlds"* (Princeton: Princeton University Press, 1984).

24. al-Dhahabī, *Mīzān* (1:430 §1606).
25. al-Suyūṭī, *Qam' al-mu'āriḍ bi nuṣrat Ibn al-Fāriḍ* [The taming of the objector with the vindication of Ibn al-Fāriḍ] in his *Maqāmāt* (2:917–918) and as quoted by Imam al-Lacknawī in *al-Raf' wal-takmīl fīl-Jarḥ wal-ta'dīl* (p. 319–320)
26. See discussion in our monograph, *Albānī and His Friends*.
27. Its chain is weak (*ḍa'īf*) as stated by the editor of al-Bayhaqī's *al-Asmā' wal-ṣifāt*. Even if it were sound, it is not traced back to the Prophet ﷺ but would be a *mawqūf* narration halted at Abū Mūsā ؓ furthermore its chain is broken (*munqaṭi'*), as the *tābi'ī* who relates it, 'Umāra b. 'Umayr, did not meet Abū Mūsā al-Ash'arī. Finally, the scholars of hadith agree that none of the narrations that mention the groaning is authentic. The preferred explanation of the *kursī* according to many of the *salaf* is Ibn 'Abbās's report: "It means His knowledge." Narrated *marfū'* from the Prophet ﷺ by Sufyān al-Thawrī with a sound chain according to Ibn Ḥajar in *Fatḥ al-bārī* (1959 ed. 8:199) and al-Ṭabarānī in *al-Sunna*; and *mawqūf* from Ibn 'Abbās by al-Ṭabarī with three sound chains in his *Tafsīr* (3:9–11), al-Māwardī in his *Tafsīr* (1:908), al-Suyūṭī in *al-Durr al-manthūr* (1:327), al-Shawkānī in *Fatḥ al-qadīr* (1:245), and others. Al-Ṭabarī chooses it as the most correct explanation: "The external wording of the Qur'an indicates the correctness of the report from Ibn 'Abbās that it [the *kursī*] is His *'ilm* [...] and the original sense of *al-kursī* is *al-'ilm*." Also narrated in "suspended" form (*mu'allaq*) by al-Bukhārī in his *Ṣaḥīḥ* from Sa'īd b. Jubayr (Book of *Tafsīr*, chapter on the saying of God, the Most High: *And if you go in fear, then (pray) standing or on horseback* (Qur'an 2:239). Its chains are documented by Ibn Ḥajar in *Taghlīq al-ta'līq* (2/4:185–186) where he shows that Sufyān al-Thawrī, 'Abd al-Raḥmān b. Mahdī, and Wakī' narrated it *marfū'* from the Prophet ﷺ, although in the *Fatḥ* he declares the *mawqūf* version from Ibn 'Abbās more likely.
28. In *al-Asmā' wal-ṣifāt* (2:197, 2:297).
29. In *Fatḥ al-bārī* (1959 ed. 13:414).
30. Cf. Ibn al-Athīr in *al-Nihāya fī gharīb al-ḥadīth* The *aw'āl* are also the nobility. Cf. *Lisān al-'Arab* and Fayrūzābādī's *qāmūs*, entry *w-'-l*.

31. al-Suyūṭī et al., *Sharḥ Sunan Ibn Mājah* (p. 18).
32. In *Tadrīb al-rāwī* (1:389).
33. See extensive translations in the *Encyclopedia of Islamic Doctrine* (2:143–159).
34. al-Kattānī, al-Yumnu wal-is'ād bi-mawlidi khayr al-'ibād (p. 24).
35. al-Suyūṭī, *al-Maṣābīḥ fī ṣalāt al-tarāwīḥ* (p. 14).
36. al-Suyūṭī, *al-Taḥadduth bi-ni' mat Allāh* (p. 150).
37. al-Suyūṭī, *al-Radd 'alā man akhlada ilā al-ard* (p. 116).
38. In *al-Taḥadduth bi-ni'mat Allāh* (p. 151).
39. "We did not see any of our shaykhs differ over the fact that Ibn Daqīq al-'Īd is the scholar of learning sent at the onset of the seventh century and alluded to in the prophetic hadiṭh" Ibn al-Subkī, *Ṭabaqāt al-shāfi'iyya al-kubrā* (9:209).
40. al-'Aẓīm Ābādī, *'Awn al-ma'būd* (4:182). Note that al-Lacknawī authored three books—in print—in refutation of certain errors committed by al-Qinnawjī: (i) *Ibrāz al-ghay al-wāqi' fī shifā' al-ghay;* (ii) *Tadhkirat al-rāshid bi-radd tabṣirat al-nāqid*; and (iii) *Tanbīh arbāb al-khibra 'alā musāmaḥāt mu'allif al-ḥiṭṭa.*

The Remembrance of God

1. al-Bukhārī (6:2694 §6970), Muslim (4:2061 §2675), al-Tirmidhī (5:581 §3603), Ibn Mājah (2:1255 §3822), Aḥmad (2:413 §9340, 2:482 §10258), and others.
2. A reference to the saying of God Most High: O *you who believe! Celebrate the praises of God, and do so often; and glorify Him morning and evening* (Qur'an 33:41–42). Narrated from Jābir by 'Abd b. Humayd (p. 333 §1107), Abū Ya'lā (3:390 §1865, 4:106 §2138), al-Bazzār (§3064), al-Ṭabarānī in *al-Awsaṭ* (3:67 §2501) and elsewhere, al-Ḥākim (1:494 = 1:671 §1820 *ṣaḥīḥal-isnād* but al-Dhahabī said one of its narrators is weak), al-Bayhaqī in the *Shu'ab* (1:397–398 §528) and elsewhere, and others. Al-Mundhirī (2:323 §2264 = 2:261 §2325) declares it fair (*hasan*). Some versions add: "Therefore, look into yourselves. He who wishes to know his rank in the eyes of God the Almighty should first look into himself as to how he himself estimates God the Almighty. God the Almighty grants His servant a rank corresponding to his estimation of God the Almighty."

3. al-Bukhārī (5:2353 §6045), Muslim (4:2069 §2689), Aḥmad (2:382 §8960 etc.), al-Ḥākim (1:495 = 1:672 §1821 *ṣaḥīḥ*,) and others.
4. Muslim (4:2074 §2700), Ibn Mājah (2:1245 §3791), Ahmad (3:92 §11893), and others.
5. Muslim (4:2075 §2701), al-Tirmidhī (5:460 §3379), al-Nasā'ī (8:249 §5426), Ahmad (4:92), and others.
6. 'Abd b. Humayd (p. 289 §925), Ahmad (3:68 §11671 and 3:71 §11692), Abū Ya'lā (2:521 §1376), al-Tabarānī in *al-Du'ā'* (p. 521), Ibn Hibbān (3:99 §817), al-Hākim (1:499 = 1:677 §1839 *sahīh al-isnād*), al-Bayhaqī in *Shu'ab al-īmān* (1:397 §526) and *al-Da'awāt al-kabīr* (1:17 §21), and others, all of them through Darrāj Abū al-Samh, from Abū al-Haytham: a weak link cf. al-Haythamī (10:75–76). Al-Nawawī did not include it in his *Adhkār*, and both Ibn 'Adī and al-Dhahabī consider this report "disclaimed" (*munkar*). Yet al-Munāwī in *Fayd al-qadīr* (2:85) and al-Shawkānī in *Tuhfat al-dhākirīn* (p. 32) say that Ibn Hajar declares it "fair" (*hasan*) in his *Amālī* and thus also does al-Suyūtī mark it in *al-Jāmi' al-ṣaghīr* (§1397), however, Ibn Hajar's *Amālī* on al-Nawawī's *Adhkār* titled *Natā'ij al-afkār* (1:97) show a weak grading for the selfsame chain. Nevertheless, the hadith is good for meritorious deeds. Al-Ghumārī mentions in *al-Mudāwī li-'ilal al-munāwī* (2:164) that the Moroccan saint Abū 'Abd Allāh Muhammad b. 'Alī al-Zuwāwī al-Bijā'ī authored a monograph titled *'Unwān ahl al-sayr al-masūn wa-kashf 'awrāt ahl al-mujūn bimā fataha Allāhu bihi min fawā'idi hadīth udhkurū Allāhạ* hattā *yaqūlū majnūn* in which he listed no less than one hundred and sixty-six benefits to this hadith alone. Note that the author of the "*al-Muhaddith*" computerized compilation in a footnote to this hadith in the file for *Fay dal-qadīr* rejects al-Suyūtī's conclusion that loud *dhikr* in the mosques is permissible on the grounds that it contradicts the hadith "Keep away from your mosques your young boys, madmen, buying and selling, quarrels, loud voices, execution of penal sentences (*ḥudūd*), and drawing of swords. Put your latrines (*maṭāhir*) at their doors and incense them on the days of *Jumu'a*." The latter report is narrated by Ibn Mājah in his *Sunan* with a chain containing a discarded narrator, an unknown, and a third weak narrator while al-Ṭabarānī's chain contains two discarded narrators and one unknown as shown in *Fatḥ al-bārī*, *Talkhīṣ al-ḥabīr*, *al-'ilal al-mutanāhiya*, *al-Asrār al-marfū'a*, etc. Al-Bayhaqī declared it *munkar* and inauthentic in his *Sunan* (10:103). In addition, the sunna establishes

that boys prayed in the mosque in Madīna behind the men and before the women. A further clue of forgery is the continuation "place your latrines at their entrances." Finally, how could such important directives touching the places and ethics of worship of the *umma* be known only to one or two singular strings of dubious narrators? At any rate, such a very weak or forged hadith cannot be used to invalidate a hadith that is merely weak although neither of them is strong enough to independently support a legal ruling, and God knows best.

7. Ibn al-Mubārak in *al-Zuhd* (p. 362 §1022) and, through him, 'Abd Allāh b. Aḥmad in *al-Zuhd* (p. 108) and al-Bayhaqī in the *Shu'ab* (1:397 §527), all of them *mursal* while al-Ṭabarānī in *al-Kabīr* (12:169 §12786) and, through him, Abū Nu'aym (3:81) narrate it from Abū al-Jawzā', from Ibn 'Abbās with a connected but weak chain per al-Haythamī (10:76) and al-Suyūṭī in the *Jāmi' al-ṣaghīr* (§903).
8. al-Tirmidhī (5:532 §3510 *ḥasan gharīb*), Aḥmad (3:150 §12545), Abū Ya'lā (6:155 §3432), Abū Nu'aym (6:268), and al-Bayhaqī in the *Shu'ab* (1:398 §529). Ibn Ḥajar cited it in *Fatḥ al-bārī* (11:210) and al-Suyūṭī marked it *ṣaḥīḥ* in the *Jāmi' al-ṣaghīr* (§859). The same is narrated from Abū Hurayra by al-Tirmidhī (5:532 §3509 *ḥasan gharīb*); Jābir by the narrators of note 2 above and by Ibn Manī' in his *Musnad* cf. Ibn Ḥajar, *al-Maṭālib al-'āliya* and *Natā'ij al-afkār* (1:22); also from Ibn 'Abbās by al-Ṭabarānī in *al-Kabīr* (11:95 §11158) with a chain containing an unnamed narrator cf. al-Haythamī (1:126); Ibn 'Umar through Mālik by Abū Nu'aym (6:354); and Mu'ādh by Ibn Abī Shayba (6:58 §29458 and 7:171 §35059) and, through him, al-Ṭabarānī in *al-Kabīr* (20:157 §326) and Ibn 'Abd al-Barr in *al-Tamhīd* (6:58). Abū Yūsuf in his *Āthār* (p. 217 §959) narrates it as a saying of Ibn Mas'ūd with the addition: "These are not the gatherings of the storytellers but the gatherings of the people of *fiqh*!"
9. The full wording is, "They both are full of goodness but these teach *fiqh* and I was but sent as a teacher (*innamā bu'ithtu mu'alliman*)." Then he sat with the latter group. Some versions have: "These are better and with them is what is needed!" Narrated from 'Abd Allāh b. 'Amr b. al-'Āṣ by al-Dārimī (3:64–66 §365), Ibn Mājah (1:83 §229), al-Bazzār (6:428 §2458), Ibn al-Mubārak in *al-Zuhd* (p. 488–489 §1388), through him al-Ṭayālisī (p. 298 §2251) and al-Ḥārith in his *Musnad* (1:185 §40), both through Ibn al-Mubārak, al-Khaṭīb with four chains in *al-Faqīh wal-mutafaqqih* (1:88–90 §30–32, §34 = 1:10–11), Ibn Shāhīn in *Sharḥ madhāhib ahl*

al-sunna (p. 46), al-Bayhaqī in *al-Madkhal ilā al-sunan al-kubrā* (1:38 §462 = p. 306), and the shaykh of our teachers Muḥammad Yāsīn al-Fādānī al-Makkī in *al-'Ujāla fil-aḥādith al-musalsala* (p. 69), through al-Dārimī, all through the pious African qadi 'Abd al-Raḥmān b. Zyād b. An'um al-Afrīqī who is weak but acceptable in narrations pertaining to morals, while al-Bukhārī deems him reliable regardless. In addition, all but Ibn Mājah's chain contain 'Abd Allāh b. Rāfi' al-Tanūkhī who is also weak. Ibn Mājah's chain is through Dāwūd b. al-Zibriqān who is discarded, from Bakr b. Khunays who is weak. Cf. al-Būṣīrī, *Miṣbāḥ* (1:32), *Mīzān*, *Mughnī*, *Kāmil*, and *Taqrīb*.

10. al-Bayhaqī, *Shu'ab* (1:401 §534). Something similar is narrated from Anas by Aḥmad (3:142 §12476), Abū Ya'lā (7:167 §4141), Abū Nu'aym (3:108), al-Ṭabarānī in *al-Awsat* (2:154 §1556), Ibn 'Adī in the *Kāmil* (6:414), and others, authenticated by al-Maqdisī in his *Mukhtāra* (7:234 §2675 and 7:236 §2678), al-Mundhirī (2:260 §2320 = 2:322 §2260), and al-Haythamī (10:76). Also narrated from a third companion, Suhayl b. Ḥanẓala al-'Abshamī, by Ibn Abī Shayba (6:60 §29477 and 7:244 §35713), Aḥmad in the *Zuhd* (p. 205), al-Ṭabarānī in *al-Kabīr* (6:212 §6039), and al-Bayhaqī in the *Shu'ab* (1:454 §694–695).
11. Aḥmad (3:68 §11670, 3:76 §11740), Abū Ya'lā (2:313 §1046, 2:531 §1403), Ibn Ḥibbān (3:98 §816), al-Bayhaqī in the *Shu'ab* (1:401 §535). Al-Haythamī said (10:76), "Aḥmad narrated it with two chains, one of which is fair, likewise Abū Ya'lā." Cf. something similar also from Ibn 'Abbās in Abū Nu'aym (6:62).
12. al-Ṭabarānī in the *Kabīr* (9:103 §8542) through Sa'īd b. Manṣūr in his *Sunan*, Ibn al-Mubārak in the *Zuhd* (p. 112–113 §333), Ibn Abī Shayba (7:110 §34579), Abū al-Shaykh in *al-'Aẓama* (5:1717 §11762), Abū Nu'aym (4:242), al-Bayhaqī in the *Shu'ab* (1:401–402 §537–538), and others cf. Ibn 'Abd al-Barr, *Tamhīd* (22:331). Al-Haythamī (10:79) said al-Ṭabarānī narrates it through the narrators of the *Ṣaḥīḥ*. All narrate it broken-chained between 'Awn b. 'Abd Allāh b. 'Utba and his paternal grand-uncle Ibn Mas'ūd, as a *mawqūf* saying of the latter. The *mawqūf* is tantamount to a prophetic report when it pertains to an imperceptible matter unknowable except through revelation. See on this: Ibn Ḥajar, *al-Nukat 'alā kitāb b. al-ṣalāḥ* (2:532); Ibn Kathīr (on Ka'b al-Aḥbār and Wahb b. Munabbih) in his *Tafsīr* (3:379 on 27:41–44); al-Qārī's commentary on Ibn Ḥajar's *Sharḥ al-nukhba* entitled *Sharḥ sharḥ nukhbat al-fikar fī muṣṭalaḥāt ahl al-athar*

[Commentary on Ibn Ḥajar's commentary on his own book "Chosen thoughts on the terminology of hadith scholars" p. 548–549); al-Sakhāwī's *Fatḥ al-mughīth* (Beirut: Dār al-Imam al-Ṭabarī, 1992 1:150–151); Nūr al-Dīn 'Itr, *Manhaj al-naqd fī 'ulūm al-ḥadīth* (p. 328) and others.

13. Referring to Pharaoh and his army when they were drowned.
14. al-Ṭabarī (25:125) and Ibn Naṣr al-Marwazī in *Ta'ẓīm qadr al-ṣalāt* (1:335 §328). Something similar is narrated from Anas, from the Prophet ﷺ by al-Tirmidhī who weakens its chain (5:380 §3255), Abū Ya'lā (7:160 §4133), Abū Nu'aym (3:53), and al-Baghawī in *Ma'ālim al-tanzīl* (4:152) cf. al-Haythamī (7:105) but al-Suyūṭī marks it *ḥasan* in *al-Jāmi' al-ṣaghīr* (§8091); and as a saying of 'Alī by Ibn al-Mubārak in *al-Zuhd* (p. 114 §336), Ibn al-Ja'd in his *Musnad* (p. 335 §2305), and Ibn Naṣr in *Ta'īm qadr al-ṣalāt* (1:334 §327). Ibn al-Jawzī cites both in his *Zād al-masīr* (7:344–345).
15. Ibn al-Mubārak in *al-Zuhd* (p. 41 §161) and Ibn Abī al-Dunyā cf. al-Tha'alibī in his *Tafsīr* (4:139–140). Abū 'Ubayd might be Ibn Abī al-Dunyā's direct teacher Abū 'Ubayd Allāh Yaḥyā b. Muḥammad b. al-Sakan or Imam al-Qāsim b. Sallām the companion of Imam Aḥmad, or someone else.
16. al-Ṭabarānī in *al-Du'ā'* (p. 523 §1869) and *al-Kabīr* (12:64 §12484), al-Bayhaqī in the *Shu'ab* (1:406 §551), and al-Bazzār with a chain al-Mundhirī (2:252 §2288 = 2:314 §2227) declared sound cf. also al-Haythamī (10:78) and al-Maqdisī who included it in the *Mukhtāra* (10:214 §225).
17. al-Bayhaqī, *Shu'ab* (1:417–418 §581), also from Zayd, from Salama b. al-Akwa', ibid. (1:417 §582). Aḥmad (4:337) narrates it through the narrators of the *Ṣaḥīḥ* cf. al-Haythamī (9:369) but with the wording "oft-repentent" (*awwāb*). Abū Nu'aym (1:121) narrates with his chain from Anas that the Prophet ﷺ defined *awwāh* as "the solitary unswerving entreater" (*al-tālī al-mutajarrid min al-'urūḍ al-khālī*). Two explanations for *awwāh* are related from Ibn Mas'ūd: [i] "the relentless maker of *du'ā'* (*al-da'ā'*)" as per Sa'īd b. Manṣūr in his *Sunan* (5:288 §1043) and Ibn Abī Shayba (6:329 §31815); and [ii] "the clement" (*al-raḥīm*) as per al-Ṭabarānī in the *Kabīr* (9:205 §9002–9003). Ibn 'Abbās reportedly glossed it as "the devotee in his prayer alone in the wilderness" per Hannād in *al-Zuhd* (2:605 §1293) and al-Ḥasan al-Baṣrī as "He whose heart hangs where God is" per al-Bukhārī in the *Tārīkh al-kabīr*

(2:326 §2635) and Ibn Ḥibbān in *al-Thiqāt* (6:180) cf. al-Bayhaqī, *Shu'ab* (5:350 §6891). The former said in his *Ṣaḥīḥ* (4:1722): "The *awwāh* is the clement in Abyssinian." In his masterpiece dictionary of Arabic and an abridgment of his larger *Lāmi'* titled *al-Qāmūs al-muḥīṭ wal-qābūs al-wasīṭ al-jāmi' limā dhahaba min kalām al-'Arabi shamāṭ īt.* [The encompassing ocean and handsome median compendium of the Arabic tongue that has gone to shreds], Imam al-Fayrūzābādī has this entry for *awwāh*: "The one who has certitude (*al-mūqin*); or the relentless supplicant (*al-da'ā'*); or the clement and soft-hearted (*al-raḥīm al-raqīq*); or the learned and wise (*al-faqīh*); or the believer (*al-mu'min*) in Abyssinian." Al-Qurṭubī lists no less than fifteen different meanings in his *Tafsīr* (verse 9:114)!

18. Dhūl-Bijādayn means "two-piece garment." His full name was 'Abd Allāh b. 'Abd Nahm (cf. *Iṣāba, Istī'āb*) and the Prophet ﷺ bore witness that he loved God and His Prophet ﷺ cf. *Shu'ab al-īmān* (1:417 §583).
19. Aḥmad (4:159) and al-Ṭabarānī in *al-Kabīr* (17:295 §813), both with a fair chain per al-Haythamī (9:369), and al-Bayhaqī in the *Shu'ab* (1:416 §580).
20. al-Ḥākim (1:522 §1361). There is another excellent report from Abū Dharr showing the prophetic praise for an *awwāh* from Najd whom the Prophet ﷺ himself buried during the campaign of Tabūk as narrated by 'Abd al-Razzāq (3:522 §6559) cf. Ibn Ḥajar, *Fatḥ al-bārī* (6:389). In yet another report the Prophet ﷺ applies the attribute *awwāha* in the feminine to our mother Zaynab bint Jahsh as narrated from our mother Maymūna bint al-Ḥārith by Abū Nu'aym (2:52–53) and Ibn 'Abd al-Barr in *al-Istī'āb* (4:1852) cf. al-Dhahabī, *Siyar* (2:217). Ibn Sa'd (3:170) narrates it as a saying of our liege-lord 'Alī about our liege-lord Abū Bakr رضي الله عنه.
21. Aḥmad (4:124 and 6:425), al-Ṭabarānī in *al-Kabīr* (7:289 §7163) and *Musnad al-shāmiyyīn* (2:157–158 §1103–1104), al-Bazzār (7:156–157 §2717 and 8:408 §3483), al-Ḥākim (1:679 §1844), and others. Al-Haythamī (1:19) said the narrators in Aḥmad's first chain are trustworthy while al-Mundhirī (2:267–268 §2351 = 2:330 §2288) declared his chain fair.
22. Abū Nu'aym (6:268) and al-Bazzār with a fair chain according to al-Haythamī (10:77) while Hannād in the *Zuhd* (p. 286) narrates something similar *mursal* from al-Ḥasan al-Baṣrī. Ibn Ḥajar cites both reports in the *Fatḥ* (11:213), which means he considers them acceptable as per the criterion he stated in his introduction. The wording is established as authentic from beginning to end.

23. al-Ṭabarī (15:235). Al-Haythamī (7:21) says al-Ṭabarānī narrates it with a chain of the narrators of the *Ṣaḥīḥ*. Al-Ṭabarānī, Ibn Qāni', and Ibn Abī Dāwūd counted 'Abd al-Raḥmān b. Sahl b. Ḥunayf among the companions while Ibn Mandah, al-'Askarī and others considered him a *tābi'ī*. Ibn Ḥajar in the *Iṣāba* (5:38) mentions some of the above as well as the report and concludes it is possible he saw the Prophet ﷺ. If he is a companion but narrates nothing from the Prophet ﷺ then his report is a companion-*mursal*, a link considered sound by agreement. The report is confirmed by similar narrations from Abū Sa'īd al-Khudrī in al-Bayhaqī's *Shu'ab* (7:334–335 §10491) and Abū al-Dardā' in Abū Nu'aym (1:345).
24. Al-Ḥākim (1:210 §419) with a strong chain of *Ṣaḥīḥ* narrators: from Thābit b. Aslam al-Bunānī, from Abū 'Uthmān al-Nahdī *mursal,* however, the latter is established as narrating from Salmān in the two *Ṣaḥīḥs* and *Sunan* hence al-Dhahabī confirmed al-Ḥākim's grading of *ṣaḥīḥ*. Abū Nu'aym's (1:342) chain is missing Abū 'Uthmān.
25. *al-Targhīb wal-tarhīb* by the *ḥāfiẓ* and imam Abū al-Qāsim Ismā'īl b. Muḥammad b. al-Faḍl al-Qurashī al-Taymī al-Asbahānī, Qawwām al-Sunna (d. 535 AH), God have mercy on him and all the pure-hearted scholars, one of those who authored the *Dalā'il al-nubuwwa.*
26. Abū Nu'aym (1:366–367) and al-Bayhaqī, *Shu'ab* (6:492–493 §9024). Narrated with the much more widespread wording "Keep your tongue moist with the *dhikr* of Allah" from 'Abd Allāh b. Busr by al-Tirmidhī (5:458 §3375 *ḥasan gharīb*), al-Ḥākim (1:672 §1822 *ṣaḥīḥ al-isnād*), and others. This great hadith is the elucidation of the hadith from Mu'ādh: "Shall I not inform you of the mainstay of this whole affair? Control this!" as he ﷺ held his tongue (§29 of al-Nawawī's *Forty*).
27. Al-Bayhaqī in the *Shu'ab* (1:409 §559) in this wording while others narrate the final sentence as "dearer to me than to free four (or eight) slaves from the descendents of Ismā'īl" cf. Abū Dawūd (3:324 §3667), Abū Ya'lā (6:119 §3392, 7:128 §4087, 7:154 §4125–4126) as per al-Haythamī (10:105), al-Ṭabarānī in *al-Awsaṭ* (6:137–138 §6022) and *al-Du'ā'* (p. 524–525 §1878–1880), al-Ṭayālisī (1:281 §2104), Abū Nu'aym (3:35), al-Bayhaqī in the *Sunan* (8:38, 8:79) and *Shu'ab* (1:409–410 §560–562), and others, an authentic report per al-Maqdisī who included it in the *Mukhtāra* (7:32–34 §2418–2419). Also narrated with variant wordings from 'Alī by 'Abd al-Razzāq (1:530 §2027), al-'Abbās by al-Bazzār

(4:127 §1299), Sahl b. Sa'd by al-Ṭabarānī in *al-Awsaṭ* (8:348–349 §8836) and others, Abū Hurayra by Isḥāq b. Rāhūyah in his *Musnad* (1:371 §384) and al-Ṭabarānī in *al-Du'ā'* (p. 525 §1881), and Abū Umāma by al-Ṭabarānī in *al-Kabīr* (8:260 §8013 and 8:265 §8028) and *al-Du'ā'* (p. 525 §1882). Another wording from Abū Umāma specifies that the *dhikr* consists in *takbīr*, *taḥmīd*, *tasbīḥ*, and *tahlīl* in Aḥmad (5:253 §22239, 5:255 §22248, 5:261 §22308) with a fair chain per al-Haythamī (10:104). Also narrated *mawqūf* from Mu'ādh and 'Ubāda b. al-Ṣāmit by Ibn Abī Shayba (6:58–59 §29458, §29470, 7:170 §35048, 7:172 §35070).

28. al-Bukhārī (1:288 §805-806), Muslim (1:410 §583), Aḥmad (1:367 §3478), Ibn Khuzayma (3:102 §1707), and 'Abd al-Razzāq (2:245 §3225). Imam al-Nawawī said in *Sharḥ ṣaḥīḥ Muslim* (5:84): "This is evidence for what some of the earlier generations (*salaf*) said, namely, that it is desirable (*mustaḥabb*) to raise the voice with *takbīr* and *dhikr* directly following the obligatory prayers. Among the later scholars who also declared it desirable is Ibn Ḥazm al-ẓāhirī."

29. al-Tirmidhī through two different chains (5:491 §3428–3429 *gharīb*), al-Dārimī (2:379 §2692), Aḥmad (1:47 §327), al-Bazzār (1:238 §125), al-Ṭayālisī (1:4 §12), 'Abd b. Ḥumayd (1:39 §28), al-Ṭabarānī in *al-Kabīr* (12:300 §13175) and *al-Du'ā'* (p. 251–252 §789–793), al-Rāmahurmuzī in *al-Muḥaddith al-fāṣil* (p. 332–333), al-Ḥākim (1:721–722 §1974) and from Ibn 'Umar also (1:722–723 §1975–1976 *isnād ṣaḥīḥ 'alā sharṭ* al-shaykhayn but al-Dhahabī demurred), and al-Baghawī in *Sharḥ al-Sunna* (5:132–133 §1338 *ḥasan gharīb*). Al-Qārī said in *al-Asrār al-marfū'a* (p. 329–330 §486): "Ibn Qayyim al-Jawziyya said this hadith was defective and the imams of hadith declared it defective. Al-Tirmidhī mentioned it in his *Jāmi'* then said it is singular (*gharīb*). Ibn Abī Ḥātim said, 'I asked my father about this and he told me it is a disclaimed (*munkar*) hadith containing many mistakes.' Ibn Mājah narrated it in his *Sunan* but there is weakness in its chain as per al-Dāraquṭnī, al-Nasā'ī, al-Dārimī, and Abū Zur'a. Ibn Ḥibbān said [of 'Amr b. Dīnār Qahrumān Āl al-Zubayr]: 'It is not lawful to write his narrations except to marvel! He used to single himself out in attributing forgeries to the top trustworthy narrators; and God knows best the truth of all situations.'" However, it has other chains that do not include 'Amr b. Dīnār Qahrumān, in light of which the authorities strengthened this hadith cf. al-Mundhirī in *al-Targhīb* (2:337 §2619 = 3:8 §2551 *isnāduhu muttaṣil ḥasan*), al-Dhahabī in the *Siyar* (*Risāla* ed. 17:498–499 *isnād ṣāliḥ*

gharīb), and al-Shawkānī in *Tuḥfat al-dhākirīn* ("*ḥasan* at the very least") while al-Maqdisī included it in the *Mukhtāra* (1:296–298 §186–188) which reconciles Shu'ayb al-Arna'ūṭ's conclusion that all its chains are very weak in his edition of the *Musnad* (1:410–413 §327) with his statement that "it has other paths that strengthen it" in his edition of al-Baghawī's *Sharḥ al-sunna* (5:132), and God knows best.

30. *Muwaṭṭa'* (1:334 §736), Abū Dāwūd (2:162 §1814), Aḥmad (4:55-56), Ibn Mājah (2:975 §2922), and others, none of them mentioning *takbīr* but rather *tahlīl* and *talbiya*.
31. al-Fākihī, *Akhbār Makka* (3:9–10 §1704).
32. al-Bayhaqī, *Sunan* (3:312 §6061), al-Fākihī, *Akhbār Makka* (4:258–259 §2580), and al-Bukhārī (1:330) without chain cf. Ibn Ḥajar, *Taghlīq al-ta'līq* (2:378–380) and *Fatḥ al-bārī* (2:462).
33. Aḥmad (1:172 §1477, 1:180 §1559, 1:187 §1623), Abū Ya'lā (2:81 §731), 'Abd b. Ḥumayd (p. 76 §137), Ibn Abī Shayba (6:85 §29663, 7:84 §34377), al-Bayhaqī in the *Shu'ab* (1:406–407 §552, 7:296 §10369) and others from Sa'd b. Mālik; Abū Ya'lā (8:182 §4738), Ibn Abī Shayba (6:85 §29664), al-Bayhaqī in the *Shu'ab* (1:407 §555), and others from 'Ā'isha with weak chains as per al-'Irāqī in his documentation of the *Iḥyā'*, al-Munāwī in *Fayḍ al-qadīr*, al-Haythamī, and Asad in his edition of Abū Ya'lā; Ibn Ḥibbān (3:91 §809) and al-Bayhaqī in the *Shu'ab* (1:407 §554) from Sa'd b. Abī Waqqāṣ, a weak hadith according to al-Nawawī in his *Fatāwā*, al-Haythamī (10:81), and the editor of Ibn Ḥibbān's *Ṣaḥīḥ*. As for the report attributed to al-Ḥasan al-Baṣrī that "Silent *dhikr* is seventy times better than loud *dhikr*" its meaning is subject to the stipulations of sincerity, etc. outlined by al-Nawawī and others, although its chain is broken and weak, while its attribution to the Prophet ﷺ in al-Rāzī's *Tafsīr al-kabīr* is chainless.
34. Aḥmad (4:201), Abū Ya'lā (3:278 §1737), al-Bukhārī in *Khalq af'āl al-'ibād* (p. 111), and al-Ṭabarānī in *al-Kabīr* (17:334 §923) and *al-Awsaṭ* (3:304 §3235), all of them from 'Uqba b. 'Āmir. Also from him but in reverse order of wording, al-Tirmidhī (5:180 §2919 *ḥasan gharīb*), Aḥmad (4:151, 4:158), Ibn Ḥibbān (3:8 §734), and others. Also narrated from Mu'ādh by al-Bayhaqī in the *Shu'ab* (2:384 §2131).
35. al-Nawawī, *Adhkār* (chapter 70 "Tilāwat al-Qur'ān"), *Fatāwā* (p. 274–275), and *Sharḥ ṣaḥīḥ Muslim* (17:16).
36. Cf. al-Qurṭubī, *Tidhkār* (p. 238–239 §120).

37. al-'Ajlūnī in *Kashf al-khafā* said that the meaning of secret *dhikr* is *tafakkur* or reflection as in the saying, "*Tafakkur* of one hour is better than worshipping seventy years." Al-Bayḍāwī also said in the first lines of *Tafsīr sūrat Maryam* that softness and loudness in *dhikr* are all the same to God but softness is of greater sincerity (*wal-ikhfā'u aktharu ikhlāṣan*). And this is the position of al-Nawawī although he otherwise prefers loud *dhikr* because it entails more *'amal* than silent *dhikr* as already cited.
38. This elaboration is taken from the *Fatāwā khayriyya* cf. al-Lacknawī's citations in *Sibāḥat al-fikr* (p. 28–29).
39. Cf. Ibn Kathīr, *Tafsīr* (3:70).
40. al-Bazzār (7:97-100 §2655) broken-chained through unknown narrators with a long *munkar* continuation according to Ibn Ḥajar cf. his notes on al-Mundhirī (1:243–245 §931 = 1:318–319 §936), al-Haythamī (2:253–254), a forgery according to al-'Uqaylī in *al-Ḍu'afā'* (2:39).
41. As narrated from Zayd b. Aslam by Ibn Abī Ḥātim and others cf. al-Suyūṭī, *Durr* (3:475–476), al-Ṭabarī (8:206–207) and others. This verse refers to the *adab* of *du'ā'* (cf. al-Ṭabarī from Ibn 'Abbās and Ibn Kathīr) which demands peace, composure, dignity, and beauty as established by the reports listed by al-Suyūṭī in *al-Durr al-manthūr,* "to keep self-display (*riyā'*) at bay" (al-Qurṭubī) and because some people used to shout in their *du'ā'* and show no restraint (Ibn Mājah and *Jalalayn*). Another Qur'anic proof for both loud and silent *dhikr* is the verse *Say: Who delivers you from the darkness of the land and the sea? You call upon Him with open fervor and in secret, saying: If we are delivered from this, we truly will be of the thankful* (Qur'an 6:63), as indicated by al-Ṭabarī and *Tafsīr al-jalālayn* while Ibn Kathīr states: *jahran wa-sirran.*
42. Cf. al-Baghawī (2:166), al-Suyūṭī (*op.cit.*), and others.
43. Aḥmad (5:55), Ibn Mājah (2:1271 §29411), Ibn Ḥibbān (15:155 §6763–6764), al-Ḥākim (1:267 §579, 1:724 §1979 *ṣaḥīḥ al-isnād*), and others.
44. Cf. Mufti Aḥmad Yār Khān in *Jā'a al-ḥaqq* (p. 337): "The verse refers to *du'ā'* and not other kinds of *dhikr*. And to make *du'ā'* softly is better, so that one may achieve total sincerity." Cf. also al-Qurṭubī's mention that the Ḥanafīs prefer to keep the *dhikr* of "*Āmīn*" secret in *ṣalāt* as well as Qur'an-recitation and *takbīr* behind the imam in prayer on the basis of that Divine command. This is patently the specific meaning meant in the prohibitions of loudness by Abū Ḥanīfa, Ibn al-Humām, al-Kāsānī, Isḥāq al-Dihlawī, al-'Aynī, Gangohī, Karghī, Qashṭānī, etc.

45. Al-Dārimī in the *Muqaddima* of his *Sunan* from al-Ḥakam b. al-Mubārak who narrates from 'Amr b. Salima al-Hamadānī, a weak (*ḍa'īf*) narrator. Ibn Ma'īn saw him and said: "His narrations are worth nothing"; Ibn Kharrāsh said: "He is not accepted"; al-Dhahabī listed him among those who are weak and whose hadith is not retained in *al-Ḍu'afā' wal-matrūkīn* (p. 212 §3229), *Mīzan al-i'tidāl* (3:293), and *al-Mughni fil-ḍu'afā'* (2:491); al-Haythamī declared him weak in *Majma' al-zawā'id*, chapter titled "Bāb al-'ummāl 'alā al-ṣadaqa." Its authenticity was questioned by al-Suyūṭī in the present fatwa in *al-Ḥāwī* (2:31); al-Ḥifnī in *Faḍl al-tasbīḥ wal-tahlīl* as cited by al-Lacknawī, and al-Lacknawī himself in *Sibāḥat al-fikr fil-jahri bil-dhikr* (p. 25 and 42–43).
46. This is 'Abd al-Raḥmān b. 'Abd Allāh b. 'Utba b. 'Abd Allāh b. Mas'ūd.
47. He is "slightly weak" (*layyin*).
48. Cited by al-Munāwī in *Fayḍ al-qadīr* (1:457), al-Nābulusī in *Jam' al-asrār* (p. 66), al-Ḥifnī in *Faḍl al-tasbīḥ wal-tahlīl* as cited in al-Lacknawī, *Sibāḥat al-fikr* (p. 25).

Appendix II

1. See note 1 p. 64
2. al-Ramlī, *Fatāwā khayriyya* (p. 180–181).
3. al-Haytamī, *Fatāwā Ḥadīthiyya* (p. 67 and p. 80).
4. I.e., the *Fatāwā bazzāziyya* (6:378).
5. I.e., according to Qadi Khān, although none of the hadith authorities declared it other than *ḍa'īf.*
6. al-Bukhārī (3:1091 §2830 etc.), Muslim (4:2076 §2704), al-Tirmidhī (5:509 §3461), Abū Dāwūd (2:87 §1526), Aḥmad (4:394 etc.) and others from Abū Mūsā al-Ash'arī. This hadith refers to the *adab* of *du'ā'* in the same way as the verse already cited from Sūrat al-A'rāf, and—by extension—*dhikr.* This is not to mean that loud *du'ā'* is not permitted but, as al-Nawawī said in *Sharḥ ṣaḥīḥ Muslim* as already quoted, that "the soft one is preferable when there is no need for loudness, and if there is a need then one uses loudness just as the narrations to that effect mention." Similarly Ibn Ḥajar in *Fatḥ al-bārī* confirms that loud *dhikr* is illustrated by the report of Ibn 'Abbās to that effect i.e., loud *dhikr* right after *ṣalāt* in the time of the Prophet ﷺ.

7. Cf. Ibn Ḥajar's rejection in the *Fatḥ* of the claim that the hadith of the Khaybar campaign proves that to recite *dhikr* and *du'ā'* in a loud voice is disliked unconditionally: "al-Bukhārī's arrangement dictates that this dislike concerns *takbīr* before battle, as for raising the voice in other contexts, we already mentioned in the "Book of *ṣalāt*" the hadith of Ibn 'Abbās that the raising of voice with *dhikr* was practiced in the time of the Prophet ﷺ when they left the obligatory prayer." Note that our liege-lord 'Alī ؓ similarly ordered his troops to observe humility and quiet speech before the battle of Ṣiffīn as cited in Ibn al-Athīr's *al-Nihāya*, under *'-n-y*.
8. From his *Ḥāshiyyat radd al-muḥtār* (Beirut: 1386 edition) 6:398. Cf. al-Lacknawī, *Sibāḥat al-fikr* (p. 30): The *Fatāwā khayriyya* said that Qadi Khān's fatwa applies only to *al-jahr al-fāḥish al-muḍirr* — "excessive, harmful loudness."
9. From Ḥiṣn Kayfā in Dyārbakr, Iraq.
10. *Durr* (Cairo ed. 1:617 = 3rd 1323 Bulaq ed. 1:463 = 1386 Beirut ed. 1:660).
11. Cf. Riyāḍ al-Māliḥ, *Fahras makhṭūṭāt al-taṣawwuf fil-maktabat al-ẓāhiriyya* (2:357–358 §1464).
12. See note 1.
13. See note 33 p. 72
14. al-Ḥalabī, *Rahṣ* (p. 58). As for the mention that the *faqīh* and sufi shaykh, Sidi Aḥmad al-Zarrūq (d. 846 AH) disapproved of the *haḍra*—the standing, moving *dhikr* practiced by the Shādhilīs—that, surely, was in his first phase, when he disapproved of many aspects of *taṣawwuf* on the grounds of external knowledge. In his second and final phase there is no such disapproval. Ibn 'Ajība narrates from his teachers' teachers, concerning Sidi al-Zarrūq, that he was an imam in *ṭarīqa* but not in *ḥaqīqa* and *dhawq*—until very late in life: "He was not granted an opening (*fatḥ*) until the last part of his life and almost left this life empty-handed, hence his frequent objections to the people of *nisba* and his hard stances and criticism of them" as stated in 'Abd Allāh al-Talīdī's al-Muṭrib bi-Dhikri Awliyā' al-Maghrib (p. 152) and "I heard Mawlāy al-'Arabī al-Darqāwī al-Ḥasanī—ؓ—say: Shaykh Zarrūq among the people of external knowledge is something big, but among the people of internal knowledge he is something small [. . .] And among the *awliyā* those of the upper levels know those below them, not the reverse."

15. al-Nābulusī's *Jam' al-asrār,* p. 92–94.
16. Cf. Riyāḍ al-Māliḥ, *Fahras makhṭūṭāt al-taṣawwuf fil-maktabat al-ẓāhiriyya* (2:333 §1433).
17. Cf. al-Qārī, *Mirqāt* (9:345 §5450 *Fitan*, 2nd section).
18. *Sibāḥat al-fikr* (p. 31).
19. Gangohī, *Fatāwā rashīdiyya* (Delhi ed. 1:54).
20. Ibn 'Ābidīn, *Ḥāshiyya* (Beirut ed. 6:398).
21. *Ḥāshiyyat marāqī al-falāḥ* (p. 214–215).
22. al-Bukhārī (1:179 §458) and al-Bayhaqī in the *Sunan* (2:447 §4143 and 10:103).
23. *Fatḥ al-bārī* (1:561).
24. al-Tirmidhī (4:494 §2210 *gharīb,* 4:495 §2211 *gharīb*).
25. Ibn Ḥibbān (4:529 §1651).
26. See note 9, p. 66.

Appendix III

1. al-Tirmidhī (5:696 §3862 *ḥasan gharīb*), Aḥmad (5:54, 5:57, 5:390 §23367) with three good chains, al-Bukhārī in the *Tārīkh* (5:131 §389), al-Rūyānī in his *Musnad* (2:92 §882), Abū Nu'aym (8:287), al-Bayhaqī in the *Shu'ab* (2:191 §1511) and *al-I'tiqād* (p. 321), and others. Al-Suyūṭī declared it fair (*ḥasan*) in *al-Jāmi' al- ṣaghīr* (§1442). The term *ḥasan* is missing from some editions of al-Tirmidhī but others mention it cf. al-Talīdī, *Faḍā'il al- ṣaḥāba* (p. 60n1).
2. Abū Dāwūd (2:87 §1525), Ibn Mājah (2:1277 §3882), Ibn Abī Shayba (6:20 §29152), and others.
3. Ibn Ḥibbān (3:145 §864), al-Bayhaqī in the *Sunan* (6:166–168 §10483–10493), al-Ṭabarānī in *al-Awsaṭ* (5:271–272 §5290) cf. al-Haythamī (10:137), and others.
4. Both in Muslim (1:131 §148), al-Tirmidhī (4:492 §2207), Aḥmad (3:107 etc.), and others.
5. *Sharḥ Ṣaḥīḥ Muslim* (2:178 = Dār al-Qalam ed. vol. 1/2 p. 537).
6. Aḥmad b. Taymiyya, *Majmū' al-fatāwā* (10:396–397, 10:556–562). He actually says, "If a person repeated a million times the name of God he would still not become a believer nor merit reward from God nor His paradise."

7. Ibn Mājah (1:53 §150) through trustworthy narrators cf. al-Būṣīrī, *Miṣbāḥ* (1:23); Aḥmad (1:404 §3832), al-Ḥākim (3:320 §5238 *ṣaḥīḥ al-isnād*), Ibn Ḥibbān (15:558 §7083), Ibn Abī Shayba (6:396 §32333 etc.), Abū Nu'aym (1:148-149), al-Bayhaqī in the *Shu'ab* (2:239 §1629), and others.
8. al-Tirmidhī (5:211 §2969, 5:374 §3247, 5:456 §3372), Abū Dāwūd (2:76 §1479), Ibn Mājah (2:1258 §3828), Aḥmad (4:267, 4:271, 4:276), and others.
9. Adel M. A. Abbas, *His Throne Was on Water* (p. 81).
10. This *dhikr* of the heart is the *dhikr* of the Naqshbandi path. The modalities about *dhikr* that follow are identical to those practiced in the Naqshbandi path.
11. It is related that Shaykh al-'Arabī al-Darqawī said: "It is better for one to mention God once, pray one prayer, or recite one sura or the like of that with the state of the Shariah of Muḥammad ﷺ than to do it a thousand times with the blameworthy state which is intense thirst for this world and devotion to idle talk, and absorption in misguidance. God save us!"
12. *Iḥyā' 'ulūm al-dīn* (3:19–20).

BIBLIOGRAPHY

'Abd b. Ḥumayd. *al-Muntakhab min musnad 'Abd b. Ḥumayd*. Eds. Subḥī al-Badrī al-Sāmirā'i and Maḥmūd al-Sa'īdī. Cairo: Maktabat al-Sunna, 1988.

'Abd al-Razzāq. *al-Muṣannaf.* 11 vols. Ed. Ḥabīb al-Raḥmān al-A'ẓamī. Beirut: al-Maktab al-Islāmī, 1983. With Ma'mar b. Rāshid al-Azdī's *Kitāb al-jāmi'* as the last two volumes.

Abū Dāwūd al-Sijistānī. *Sunan*. 3 vols. Ed. Muḥammad Fu'ād 'Abd al-Bāqī. Beirut: Dār al-Kutub al-'Ilmiyya, 1996.

Abū Dāwūd al-Ṭayālisī. See al-Ṭayālisī.

Abū Nu'aym al-Aṣbahānī. *Ḥilyat al-awliyā' wa-ṭabaqāt al-asfiya'*. 10 vols. 4th ed. Beirut: Dār al-Kitāb al-'Arabī, 1985.

Abū al-Shaykh [Ibn Ḥayyān al-Aṣbahānī]. *al-'Aẓama*. 5 vols. Ed. Riḍā' Allāh al-Mubārakfūrī. Riyadh: Dār al-'Āṣima, 1988.

Abū Ya'lā al-Mawṣilī. *Musnad*. 13 vols. Ed. Ḥusayn Salīm Asad. Damascus: Dār al-Ma'mūn lil-Turāth, 1984.

Aḥmad b. Ḥanbal. *al-Musnad*. 6 vols. Cairo: Mu'assasat Qurṭuba, n.d.

——. *al-Zuhd*. Beirut: Dar al-Kutub al-'Ilmiyya, 1978.

al-'Aydarūsī, 'Abd al-Qādir. *al-Nūr al-sāfir 'an akhbār al-qarn al-'āshir.* Beirut: Dār al-Kutub al-'Ilmiyya, 1985.

al-Baghawī. *Ma'ālim al-tanzīl*. 5 vols. Ed. 'Abd al-Razzāq al-Mahdī. Beirut: Dār Iḥyā' al-Turāth al-'Arabī, 2000.

——. *Sharḥ al-sunna*. 16 vols. Eds. Shu'ayb al-Arna'ūṭ and Zuhayr al-Shāwīsh 2nd ed. Beirut: al-Maktab al-Islāmī, 1983.

al-Bayhaqī. *al-Da'awāt al-kabīr*. 2 vols. Ed. Badr b. 'Abd Allāh al-Badr. Kuwait: Markaz al-Makhṭūṭāt wal-Turāth, 1989.

——. *al-I'tiqād 'alā madhhabi al-salaf ahl al-sunnati wal-jamā'a*. Beirut: Dār al-Afāq al-Jadīda, 1981.

——. *al-Madkhal ilā al-sunan al-kubrā*. 2 vols. Ed. Muḥammad Ḍiyā' al-Raḥmān al-A'ẓamī. Kuwait: Dār al-Khulafā' lil-Kitāb al-Islāmī, 1984. 2nd ed. Riyadh: Maktabat Aḍwā' al-Salaf, 1990.

——. *Shu'ab al-īmān*. 8 vols. Ed. Muḥammad Zaghlūl. Beirut: Dār al-Kutub al-'Ilmiyya, 1990.

———. *al-Sunan al-kubrā*. 10 vols. Ed. Muḥammad ʻAbd al-Qādir ʻAṭā. Makka: Maktaba Dār al-Baz, 1994.

al-Bazzār. *al-Musnad* [*al-Baḥr al-zakhkhār*]. 9 vols. Ed. Maḥfūẓ al-Raḥmān Zayn Allāh. Beirut: Mu'assasat ʻUlūm al-Qur'ān; Madīna: Maktabat al-ʻUlūm wal-Ḥikam, 1989.

———. *Mukhtaṣar al-musnad*. See Ibn Ḥajar, *Mukhtaṣar zawā'id musnad al-Bazzār*.

al-Bukhārī, Muḥammad b. Ismāʻīl. *al-Adab al-mufrad*. Ed. Muḥammad Fu'ād ʻAbd al-Bāqī. 3rd ed. Beirut: Dār al-Bashā'ir al-Islāmiyya, 1989.

———. *Khalq af'āl al-ʻibād*. Ed. ʻAbd al-Raḥmān ʻUmayra. Beirut: Mu'assasat al-Risāla, 1990; Riyadh: Dār al-Maʻārif al-Saʻūdiyya, 1978.

———. *Ṣaḥīḥ*. 6 vols. Ed. Muṣṭafā Dīb al-Bughā. 3rd ed. Beirut: Dār Ibn Kathīr, 1987.

———. *al-Tārīkh al-kabīr*. 8 vols. Ed. al-Sayyid Hāshim al-Nadwī. Beirut: Dār al-Fikr, n.d.

al-Būṣīrī. *Miṣbāḥ al-zujāja fī zawā'id Ibn Mājah*. 4 vols. Ed. Muḥammad al-Muntaqā al-Kashnawī. 2nd ed. Beirut: Dār al-ʻArabiyya, 1983.

al-Dārimī. [*al-Musnad al-jāmiʻ*] *Fatḥ al-mannān sharḥ wa-taḥqīq kitāb al-dārimī al-musammā bil-musnad al-jāmiʻ*. 10 vols. Ed. Abū ʻĀṣim Nabīl Hāshim al-Ghamrī. Makka: al-Maktbat al-Makkiyya; Beirut: Dār al-Bashā'ir al-Islāmiyya, 1999.

———. *Musnad*. 2 vols. Ed. Fu'ād Aḥmad Zamarlī and Khālid al-Sabʻ al-ʻIlmī. Beirut: Dār al-Kitāb al-ʻArabī, 1987.

al-Dhahabī, Muḥammad Shams al-Dīn. *Siyar aʻlām al-nubalā'*. 23 vols. Ed. Shuʻayb al-Arna'ūṭ and Muḥammad Naʻīm al-ʻAraqsūsī. Beirut: Mu'assasat al-Risāla, 1992–1993.

al-Fādānī. *al-ʻUjāla fil-aḥādith al-musalsala*. 2nd ed. Damascus: Dār al-Baṣā'ir, 1985.

al-Fākihī. *Akhbār Makka fī qadīm al-dahr wa-ḥadīthih*. 6 vols. Ed. ʻAbd al-Mālik ʻAbd Allāh Duhaysh. 2nd ed. Beirut: Dār Khiḍr, 1994.

al-Ghumārī, Aḥmad b. Muḥammad b. al-Ṣiddīq. *al-Mudāwī li-ʻilal al-jāmiʻ al-ṣaghīr wa-sharḥ al-munāwī*. 6 vols. Ed. Muṣṭafā Ṣabrī. Cairo: al-Maktaba al-Makkiyya, 1996.

al-Ḥākim. *al-Mustadrak ʻalā al-ṣaḥīḥayn*. With al-Dhahabī's *Talkhīṣ al-mustadrak*. 5 vols. Indexes by Yūsuf ʻAbd al-Raḥmān al-Marʻashlī. Beirut: Dār al-Maʻrifa, 1986. Reprint of the 1334/1916 Hyderabad edition.

———. *al-Mustadrak ʻala al-ṣaḥīḥayn*. With al-Dhahabī's *Talkhīṣ al-mustadrak*. 4 vols. Annotations by Muṣṭafā ʻAbd al-Qādir ʻAṭā'. Beirut: Dār al-Kutub al-ʻIlmiyya, 1990.

al-Ḥalabī, Ibrāhīm. *al-Rahṣ wal-waqṣ li-mustaḥill al-raqṣ* Ed. Ḥasan al-Samāḥī Suwaydān and ʻAbd al-Qādir al-Arna'ūṭ. Damascus: Dār al-Bashā'ir, 2002.

Hannād b. al-Sarī al-Kūfī. *al-Zuhd*. 2 vols. Ed. ʻAbd al-Raḥmān al-Faryawā'ī. Kuwait: Dār al-Khulafā' lil-Kitāb al-Islāmī, 1986.

al-Ḥārith b. Abī Usāma. *Musnad [Bughyat al-bāḥith 'an zawā'id musnad al-ḥārith]*. 2 vols. Ed. Ḥusayn Aḥmad Ṣāliḥ al-Bākirī. Madīna: Markaz Khidmat al-Sunna wal-Sīra al-Nabawiyya, 1992.

al-Haytamī, Aḥmad. *al-Fatāwā al-ḥadīthiyya*. Cairo: Muṣṭafā al-Bābā al-Ḥalabī, Repr. 1970, 1989.

al-Haythamī, Nūr al-Dīn. *Majma' al-zawā'id wa-manba' al-fawā'id*. 10 vols. in 5. Cairo: Maktabat al-Qudsī, 1932–1934. Repr. Beirut: Dār al-Kitāb al-'Arabī, 1967, 1982, and 1987.

Ibn 'Abd al-Barr. *al-Istī'ab fī ma'rifat al-aṣḥāb*. 8 vols. in 4. Ed. 'Alī Muḥammad al-Bajawī. Beirut: Dār al-Jil, 1992.

———. *al-Tamhīd limā fil-muwaṭṭa' min al-ma'ānī wal-asānīd*. 22 vols. Eds. Muṣṭafā b. Aḥmad al-'Alawī and Muḥammad 'Abd al-Kabīr al-Bakrī. Morocco: Wizārat 'Umūm al-Awqāf wal-Shu'ūn al-Islāmiyya, 1967–1968.

Ibn Abī Shayba. *al-Muṣannaf*. 7 vols. Ed. Kamāl al-Ḥūt. Riyadh: Maktabat al-Rushd, 1989.

Ibn 'Ābidīn. *Radd al-muḥtār ḥāshiyyat al-durr al-mukhtār sharḥ tanwīr al-abṣār*. 6 vols. Bulāq: al-Maṭba'at al-Amīriyya, 1326. Also 6 vols. Beirut: Dār al-Fikr, 1966.

Ibn 'Adī. *al-Kāmil fī ḍu'afā' al-rijāl*. 7 vols. Ed. Yaḥyā Mukhtār Ghazawī. Beirut: Dār al-Fikr, 1988.

Ibn Ḥajar. *Fatḥ al-bārī sharḥ ṣaḥīḥ al-Bukhārī*. 13 vols. Ed. Muḥammad Fu'ād 'Abd al-Bāqī and Muḥibb al-Dīn al-Khaṭīb. Beirut: Dār al-Ma'rifa, 1959–1960.

———. *al-Iṣāba fī tamyīz al-ṣaḥāba*. 8 vols in 4. Ed. 'Alī Muḥammad al-Bijāwī. Beirut: Dār al-Jīl, 1992.

———. *Mukhtaṣar zawā'id musnad al-Bazzār*. 2 vols. Ed. Ṣabrī 'Abd al-Khāliq Abū Dharr. Beirut: Mu'assasat al-Kutub al-Thaqāfiyya, 1993.

———. *Natā'ij al-afkār fī takhrīj aḥādīth al-adhkār*. 3 vols. Ed. Ḥamdī 'Abd al-Majīd al-Salafī. Damascus and Beirut: Dār Ibn Kathīr, 2000.

———. *Taghlīq al-ta'līq 'alā ṣaḥīḥ al-Bukhārī*. 5 vols. Ed. Sa'īd 'Abd al-Raḥmān Mūsā al-Qizqī. 2nd ed. Beirut: al-Maktab al-Islāmī; Amman: Dār 'Ammār, 1989.

Ibn Ḥibbān. *Ṣaḥīḥ Ibn Ḥibbān bi-tartīb Ibn Balbān*. 18 vols. Ed. Shu'ayb al-Arna'ūṭ. Beirut: Mu'assasat al-Risāla, 1993.

———. *al-Thiqāt*. Also known as *Tārīkh al-thiqāt*. 9 vols. Ed. Sayyid Sharaf al-Dīn Aḥmad. N.p.: Dār al-Fikr, 1975.

Ibn al-Ja'd. *Musnad*. Ed. 'Āmir Aḥmad Ḥaydar. Beirut: Mu'assasat Nādir, 1990.

Ibn al-Jawzī. *Zād al-masīr fī 'ilm al-tafsīr*. 10 vols. 3rd ed. Beirut: al-Maktab al-Islāmī, 1984.

Ibn Kathīr. *Tafsīr al-Qur'ān al-'aẓīm*. 4 vols. Beirut: Dār al-Fikr, 1981.

Ibn Mājah. *Sunan*. Ed. Muḥammad Fu'ād 'Abd al-Bāqī. Beirut: Dār al-Fikr, n.d.

Ibn al-Mubārak. *al-Zuhd*. Ed. Ḥabīb al-Raḥmān al-A'ẓamī. Beirut: Dār al-Kutub al-'Ilmiyya, n.d.

Ibn Naṣr al-Marwazī. *Ta'ẓīm qadr al-ṣalāt*. 2 vols. Ed. 'Abd al-Raḥmān al-Faryawā'ī. Madīna: Maktabat al-Dār, 1986.

Ibn Rāhūyah. See Isḥāq b. Rāhūyah.

Ibn Sa'd. *al-Ṭabaqāt al-kubrā*. 8 vols. Beirut: Dār Sadir, n.d.

Ibn Shāhīn. *Sharḥ madhāhib ahl al-sunna*. Ed. 'Ādil b. Muḥammad. Cairo: Mu'assasat Qurṭuba-Dār al-Mishkāt, 1995.

Isḥāq b. Rāhūyah. *Musnad*. 5 vols. Ed. 'Abd al-Ghafūr 'Abd al-Ḥaqq al-Balūshī. Madīna: Maktabat al-Īmān, 1991–1995.

al-Khaṭīb al-Baghdādī. *al-Faqīh wal-mutafaqqih*. 2 vols. Ed. 'Ādil al-'Azāzī. Dammām: Dār Ibn al-Jawzī, 1997.

——. *al-Faqīh wal-mutafaqqih*. Ed. Ismā'īl al-Anṣārī. Beirut: Dār al-Kutub al-'Ilmiyya, 1980.

al-Lacknawī. *Sibāḥat al-fikri fīl-jahri bil-dhikr*. Ed. 'Abd al-Fattāḥ Abū Ghudda. 5th ed. Beirut: Dār al-Bashā'ir al-Islāmiyya, 1995.

Mālik b. Anas. *al-Muwaṭṭa'*. 2 vols. Ed. Muḥammad Fu'ād 'Abd al-Bāqī. Beirut: Dār al-Kutub al-'Ilmiyya, n.d.

al-Maqdisī. *al-Aḥādīth al-mukhtāra*. 10 vols. Ed. 'Abd al-Mālik b. 'Abd Allāh b. Duhaysh. Makka: Maktabat al-Nahḍat al-Ḥadītha, 1990.

al-Marwazī, Muḥammad b. Naṣr. *Ta'ẓīm qadr al-ṣalāt*. 2 vols. Ed. 'Abd al-Raḥmān al-Faryawā'ī. Madīna: Maktabat al-Dār, 1986.

al-Munāwī. *Fayḍ al-qadīr sharḥ al-jāmi' al-ṣaghīr*. 6 vols. Cairo: al-Maktabat al-Tijāriyyat al-Kubrā, 1356/1937. Repr. Beirut: Dār al Ma'rifa, 1972.

al-Mundhirī. *al-Targhīb wal-tarhīb*. With al-Nājī's *Awhām al-targhīb*. 5 vols. Ed. Ayman Ṣāliḥ Sha'bān. Cairo: Dār al-Ḥadīth, 1994.

——. *al-Targhīb wal-tarhīb*. 4 vols. Ed. Ibrāhīm Shams al-Dīn. Beirut: Dār al-Kutub al-'Ilmiyya, 1997.

Muslim. *Ṣaḥīḥ*. 5 vols. Ed. Muḥammad Fu'ād 'Abd al-Bāqī. Beirut: Dār Iḥyā' al-Turāth al-'Arabī, 1954. See also al-Nawawī, *Sharḥ ṣaḥīḥ Muslim*.

al-Nābulusī, 'Abd al-Ghanī. *Jam' al-asrār fī radd al-ṭa'n 'an al-ṣūfiyyat al-akhyār ahl al-tawājud bil-adhkār*. Ed. Hibat al-Māliḥ. Damascus: Dār al-Maḥabba; Beirut: Dār Āya, n.d.

al-Nasā'ī. *Sunan*. See al-Suyūṭī, *Sharḥ Sunan al-Nasā'ī*.

——. *al-Sunan al-kubrā*. 6 vols. Eds. 'Abd al-Ghaffār Sulaymān al-Bandārī and Sayyid Kusrawī Ḥasan. Beirut: Dār al-Kutub al-'Ilmiyya, 1991.

al-Nawawī. *al-Adhkār al-muntakhaba min kalām Sayyid al-Abrār*. Cairo: al-Ḥalabī 1348/1929.

——. *Fatāwā*. Ed. Muḥammad al-Ḥajjār. Aleppo: al-Maṭba'at al-'Arabiyya, 1971.

——. *Sharḥ ṣaḥīḥ Muslim*. 18 vols. Beirut: Dār Iḥyā' al-Turāth al-'Arabī, 1972.

al-Qārī. *al-Asrār al-marfū'a fil-aḥādīth al-mawḍū'a. (al-Mawḍū'āt al-kubrā)*. Ed. Muḥammad b. Luṭfī al-Ṣabbāgh. 2nd ed. Beirut and Damascus: al-Maktab al-Islāmī, 1986.

——. *Mirqāt al-mafātīḥ sharḥ mishkāt al-maṣābīḥ*. With Ibn Ḥajar's *Ajwiba 'alā risālat al-qazwīnī ḥawla ba'ḍ aḥādīth al-maṣābīḥ*. 11 vols. Ed. Ṣidqī Muḥammad Jamīl al-'Aṭṭār. Damascus: Dār al-Fikr, 1994.

al-Qurṭubī. [*Tafsīr*] *al-jāmi' li aḥkām al-Qur'ān*. 20 vols. Ed. Aḥmad 'Abd al-'Alīm al-Bardūnī. 2nd ed. Cairo: Dār al-Sha'b; Beirut: Dār Iḥyā' al-Turāth al-'Arabī, 1952–1953. Reprint.

——. *al-Tidhkār fī afḍal al-adhkār*. Ed. Yūsuf 'Alī Badyawī. Damascus and Beirut: Dār Ibn Kathīr, 1999.

al-Rūyānī. *Musnad*. 2 vols. Ed. Ayman 'Alī Abū Yamānī. Cairo: Mu'assasat Qurṭuba, 1996.

Sa'īd b. Manṣūr. *Sunan*. 2 vols. Ed. Ḥabīb al-Raḥmān al-A'ẓamī. India: al-Dār al-Salafiyya, 1982.

al-Shāfi'ī. [*Musnad*] *Tartīb musnad al-imām al-a'ẓam wal-mujtahid al-muqaddam Abī 'Abd Allāh Muḥammad b. Idrīs al-Shāfi'ī*. 2 vols. Eds. Yūsuf 'Alī al-Zawlawī al-Ḥasanī and 'Izzat 'Aṭṭār al-Ḥusaynī. Cairo: n.p., 1951. Repr. Beirut: Dār al-Kutub al-'Ilmiyya, n.d.

al-Shawkānī. *Tuḥfat al-dhākirīn bi 'uddat al-ḥiṣn al-ḥaṣīn min kalām Sayyid al-Mursalīn*. Ed. Najāḥ 'Awad Ṣiyām. Cairo: Dār al-Naṣr, n.d.

al-Suyūṭī, Jalāl al-Dīn. *al-Durr al-manthūr fil-tafsīr al-ma'thūr*. 8 vols. Beirut: Dār al-Fikr, 1994.

——. *al-Ḥāwī lil-fatāwī*. 2 vols. Ed. Muḥammad Muḥyī al-Dīn 'Abd al-Ḥamīd. 3rd ed. Cairo: al-Maktabat al-Tijāriyya al-Kubrā, 1959.

——. *Ḥusn al-muḥāḍara fī tārīkh Miṣr wal-Qāhira*. Ed. Muḥammad Abū al-Faḍl Ibrāhīm. Cairo: Dār Iḥyā' al-Kutub al-'Arabiyya, 1967.

——. *al-Jāmi' al-ṣaghīr min ḥadīth al-bashīr al-nadhīr*. 2 vols. Ed. Muḥammad Muḥyī al-Dīn 'Abd al-Ḥamīd. Damascus: Maktabat al-Ḥalbūnī, 1983.

——. *Sharḥ sunan al-Nasā'ī*. 9 vols. Ed. 'Abd al-Fattah Abū Ghudda. Aleppo and Beirut: Maktab al-Maṭbū'āt al-Islāmiyya, 1986. Includes al-Nasā'īs' *Sunan*.

——. *al-Taḥadduth bi-ni'mat Allāh*. Ed. Haytham Khalīfa Ṭu'aymī. Beirut: al-Maktabat al-'Aṣriyya, 2003.

——, 'Abd al-Ghanī al-Dihlawī, and Fakhr al-Ḥasan al-Gangohi. *Sharḥ sunan Ibn Mājah*. Karachi: Qadimi Kutub Khana, n.d. Includes Ibn Mājah's *Sunan*.

al-Ṭabarānī. *al-Du'ā'*. Ed. Muṣṭafā 'Abd al-Qādir 'Aṭā'. Beirut: Dār al-Kutub al-'Ilmiyya, 1993.

——. *al-Mu'jam al-awsaṭ*. 10 vols. Eds. Ṭāriq b. 'Awaḍ Allāh and 'Abd al-Muḥsin b. Ibrāhīm al-Ḥusaynī. Cairo: Dār al-Ḥaramayn, 1995.

———. *al-Mu'jam al-kabīr.* 20 vols. Ed. Ḥamdī b.'Abd al-Majīd al-Salafī. Mosul: Maktabat al-'Ulūm wal-Ḥikam, 1983.

———. *al-Mu'jam al- ṣaghīr.* 2 vols. Ed. Muḥammad Shakūr Maḥmūd. Beirut: al-Maktab al-Islāmī; Amman: Dār 'Ammār, 1985.

———. *Musnad al-shāmiyyīn.* 2 vols. Ed. Ḥamdī b.'Abd al-Majīd al-Salafī. Beirut: Mu'assasat al-Risāla, 1984.

al-Ṭabarī, Muḥammad b. Jarīr. *Jāmi' al-bayān fī tafsīr al-Qur'ān.* 30 vols. Beirut: Dār al-Ma'ārif, 1980; Dār al-Fikr, 1985.

al-Talīdī, 'Abd Allāh. *Faḍā'il al-ṣaḥāba wal-difā'an karāmatihim wa-bayān khaṭar mubghidīhim wal-ṭā'inīna fīhim.* Beirut: Dār Ibn Ḥazm, 1999.

al-Ṭayālisī, Abū Dāwūd. *Musnad.* Beirut: Dār al-Kitāb al-Lubnānī; Dār al-Ma'rifa; Dār al-Tawfīq, n.d. All three are offset reprints of the 1321/1903 edition of *Dā'irat al-ma'ārif al-'uthmāniyya* in Hyderabad.

al-Tha'ālibī. *Jawāhir al-hisan fī tafsīr al-Qur'ān.* 4 vols. Beirut: Mu'assasat al-A'lamī, n.d.

al-Tirmidhī. *Sunan.* 5 vols. Ed. Aḥmad Shākir and Muḥammad Fu'ād 'Abd al-Bāqī. Beirut: Dār Iḥyā' al-Turāth al-'Arabī, n.d.

al-'Uqaylī, *al-Ḍu'afā' min al-ruwāt.* 4 vols. Ed. 'Abd al-Mu'ṭī Amīn Qal'ajī. Beirut: Dār al-Kutub al-'Ilmiyya, 1984.

BIOGRAPHICAL NOTES

Sajeda Maryam Poswal holds a degree in Middle Eastern Studies from the University of Manchester. She has translated several treatises from the teachings of shaykh Abū Anīs Muḥammad Barkat 'Alī into English.

Gibril F. Haddad is a well-known Lebanese American scholar and religious leader. Schooled in England, he took his PhD degree from Columbia University in New York, before embarking on an intensive study of hadith, Islamic law and doctrine under leading authorities of the Middle East.